CRE LOADED 6.1 VERSION OF OSCOMMERCE USERS
MANUAL - SUPPLEMENT TO OSCOMMERCE USERS MANUAL

CRE Loaded 6.1 version of

osCommerce Users Manual

Current for the 6.1x Series

cre loaded 6.1 version of oscommerce users manual
supplement to oscommerce users manual
©2004, 2005 Kerry Watson
Pithy Productions, Inc.

Printed in Canada

First Printing: October, 2004
Updated: June, 2005

TRADEMARKS

WARNING AND DISCLAIMER

About the Author

The author of the osCommerce Technical Manual and osCommerce Users Manual, Kerry Watson joined the Open Source movement in 1996 consulting for Netscape as the Producer for the Netscape Navigator website. Her mission was to make Netscape accessible to everyday users, not just technical users, and she wrote plain-language tutorials such as Netscape Navigator for Internet Explorer Users and Netscape Tips & Tricks. Before that she was a vice president of NetAdvantage, an e-commerce turnkey outsourcing company like PayPal. She holds an MBA and a Bachelor's of Liberal Studies with a concentration in Sociology and Communication. Today she heads Pithy Productions, Inc., a web project management company that specializes in custom OsCommerce websites.

Dedication

This book is dedicated to my mom, Sonya Gail Lodahl: my desire to make you proud has always been the biggest motivator in my life.

Your Feedback is Appreciated

I welcome your comments! Please feel free to email me to let me know what helped and what didn't, or what you'd like to see covered in future editions.

Please note that I cannot help you with technical problems related to the topic of this book. Due to the volume of mail I receive, I might not be able to reply personally to every message.

Sincerely,

KERRY WATSON
kwatson@pithyproductions.com

Contents

Contents

CRE-Loaded 6.1 Guide

Introduction

If you want to run an easy to use, robust, full-featured osCommerce store with dozens of bells and whistles pre-installed and tested for you, get ready for a real treat.

About this book:

If you are a store owner or website developer who wants a powerful, Amazon-style online store with dozens of extra features pre-installed so you can easily administer it yourself using your browser, this book is for you.

This book is intended to be a handy guide to the *extra* features that are in CRE Loaded osCommerce 6.1. It is a supplement to the osCommerce Users Manual and osCommerce Technical Manual, NOT a replacement for those books.

NOTE: This book includes information on all releases in the 6.1x series, currently to 6.15.

What is CRE Loaded osCommerce 6.1?

CRE Loaded osCommerce 6.1 is a free, powerful, Open Source*, Amazon-like online store management program. It is a souped-up version or "derivative work" of the standard ecommerce program, osCommerce. Its powerful features can be used almost immediately by a store owner or web developer with no programming experience, because you just click the menus in the Administrative Module to set it up the way you want it, and you edit pages using an easy editor like writing emails.

CRE Loaded osCommerce 6.1 is easier to use than ever. It contains in-menu prompts and suggestions, and context-sensitive HELP. Many customer-friendly improvements have been added, such as "Purchase Without Account" and PayPal IPN, which prevents dropped sales. Many more admin improvements have been installed, such as the Super-Friendly Admin Menu, which puts ALL Admin menu links on the main Admin page so you don't have to hunt or guess where the module you want is located.

Features of Both osCommerce *and* CRE Loaded OSC 6.1 Include:

For Customers:
Set up customer accounts
Customer address books (other shipping destinations)
Order history
Shopping carts—both Temporary (not logged on) and permanent (logged on)
Search the catalog for products or manufacturers
Product reviews written by customers

---

* "Open Source" software is software whose code is available for users to look at and modify freely. Many popular Internet programs are open source, including Linux, PHP, MySQL and Apache servers.

E-mail notification of new products
Number of products in each category listed
Bestseller lists
Display customers who bought this also bought...

For Shop Owners:
User-friendly administration using your web browser
Add/Edit/Remove categories, products, manufacturers, customers, and reviews
Statistics for products and customers
Tax zones, classes, and rates
Payment and shipping modules link to popular payment processors and shippers
Multi-Currency and Multi-Languages
Backup tool

CRE Loaded osCommerce 6.1's Powerful *Additional* Features Include:

More than 50 powerful extra features are pre-installed for you in CRE Loaded osCommerce 6.1. These features are called "Contributions" because they are contributed for free under the GNU Public License. See the next chapter for a complete list of additional features, what they do and where they are located. Note, these contributions are customized to work well with the other contributions in this program.

History of CRE Loaded

Ian Wilson started the first "loaded" project in late 2000. Chain Reaction Web was involved in the main osCommerce support community and sponsored the project by providing web hosting.

As Ian made new releases, Chain Reaction Web grew to take on custom programming work with osCommerce and hired Ian to do the work. This gave a financial boost to the project, and to CRE as its sponsor. As time went on CRE gave feedback to Ian, and began hosting more and more osCommerce sites. The feedback from their customers' experience, and from their role in actively supporting the issues that arose from the loaded project, gave a further dimension to its development. It was developed with feedback and ease of installation and support as important goals.

Around the time of CRE osCommerce Loaded 4, the development team wanted to give the product a brand name so they tried various names like the Neutron Edition. The product had no name other than "Ian's Loaded" well into version 5, or Loaded 5. Loaded 5 was a major upgrade because it was based on the new osCommerce MS1 that was released. That was the last loaded version Ian did before moving on and starting his own company, Zen-Cart.

When osCommerce MS2 came out, Ian introduced some energized osc enthusiasts and helped them take over the endeavor from Ian. The new volunteers looked to Chain Reaction Web for guidance in a way that the originator, Ian, had not. So Salvatore Iozzia, owner of Chain Reaction Hosting, stepped and began directing the development of the Loaded 6. Chain Reaction Web is now the developer, and not just the sponsor of the project.

What kind of skills does a user need to use CRE Loaded osCommerce 6.1?

You do not need any special skills to use CRE Loaded osCommerce 6.1. The many additions to the program make it so you will rarely or never need to edit, or know, any code.

If you do have special skills, such as experience using standard osCommerce and/or experience with HTML or PHP, you will find CRE Loaded osCommerce 6.1 a real treat. You can ultra-customize the program for you and/or your clients. But it is not necessary.

Tips for using this book:

1. Plan to start your first CRE Loaded OsCommerce 6.1 store either by having it installed for you for FREE by a web host that SPECIALIZES in osCommerce web hosting such as Chain Reaction Web – the creators of CRE Loaded - or with as close to the standard, or "default" configuration as possible.

2. If you decide to do it yourself, whether you are a store owner new to the Internet or a programmer with many years of experience, **fill out the Pre-Setup Checklist** completely before you install any CRE Loaded OsCommerce 6.1 website. This will allow you to have all the information about the website in one place. This will save you many, many hours of back-and-forth figuring out little, "just-one-more" things that were staring you in the face all along.

3. Turn to Chapter 2, Quick Reference, to easily locate the directions for the feature you want.

4. If you are in a hurry, follow the user instructions in the Action Summary to quickly work through setting up and using the feature. Otherwise follow the screen-by-screen detail for using each feature.

5. If you are serious about osCommerce, we of course recommend that you get the complete osCommerce Manuals library from www.oscommercemanuals.com.

Icons used in this book:

I have used a number of special icons to make using this book easier. They are as follows:

TIP: This is something important that will make your project much easier.

CAUTION: Follow directions exactly, this is easy to mess up!

TECHNICAL STUFF: Unless you love the technical stuff, this is something that a programmer or technical person should do for you.

DANGER, WILL ROBINSON! Don't do this unless you really, really, really know what you are doing!

Chapter

2

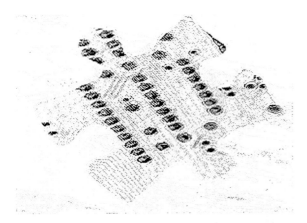

Quick Reference

In this chapter:

A Quick Reference Chart showing the features of CRE Loaded vs. basic osCommerce, a List of Contributions in CRE Loaded and their menu locations.

Quick Reference Main Admin Menu

The underlined items on this menu are features unique to CRE Loaded and are covered in detail in this book. Non-underlined items are basic features covered in the companion book, the osCommerce Users Manual.

Store Setup

 **Configuration**

My Store
Min Values
Max Values
Image Configuration
Customer Details
Default Shipping
Settings
Product Listing
Stock Control
Logging

Cache
Email
Download Manager
GZip
Sessions
WYSIWYG Editor 1.7
Affiliate Program
Site Maintenance
Purchase Without Account
Links Manager

 Locations/Taxes

Countries
Zones
Tax Zones
Tax Classes
Tax Rates

Localization

Currencies
Languages
Orders Status

Store Management

 **My Account**

My Account/Password   Log Off

Catalog

Categories/Products
Products Attributes
Manufacturers
Reviews
Easy Populate Adv.
Easy Populate Basic

Specials
Shop by Price
Cross Sell Products
SaleMaker
Featured Products
Products Expected

 Customers/Orders

Customers
Orders

Create New Account
Create new Order

 Reports

Products Viewed
Monthly Sales/Tax

Products Purchased
Customer Orders-
Total

Super-Friendly Admin Menu contribution by Kerry Watson

Tools

Backup
Banners
Cache Control
Define Languages
Email Customers

Newsletter Manager
Server Info
Who's Online

Modules

Payment
Shipping
Order Total

Affiliates
Summary
Affiliates
Payment
Sales

Clicks
Banners
Contact

Administrator

Member Groups
Update Account
File Access

FAQDesk
Faqdesk Mgmt
Reviews Mgmt
Listing Settings
FrontPage Settings

Reviews Settings
Sticky Settings
Other Settings

Design Controls

Template Admin
Infobox Admin

Coupon/Voucher
Discount Coupons
Send Gift Voucher

Gift Voucher Redeem
Gift Voucher's Sent

Info System

Info Manager
Define MainPage

Paypal IPN

Transactions
Send Test IPN

NewsDesk
Articles Mgmt
Reviews Mgmt
Listing Settings

FrontPage Settings
Reviews Settings
Sticky Settings

Links Manager

Links
Link Categories

Links Contact

List of Contributions in CRE 6.1, Their Descriptions & Locations:

Name of Contribution	What it Does for You	MAIN Menu Location
Admin With Access Levels 2.2	Assign different access and passwords to different administrators	Administrator-Member Groups
All-Products v2.4	Lists all products on one page; customer- and search-engine-friendly	Design Controls – InfoBox Admin
All Products v3.0	Lists all products sorted by category	Design Controls – InfoBox Admin
All products and manufacturers	Lists all products sorted by manufacturer	Design Controls – InfoBox Admin
Attribute_Sorter_Copierv5.1	Makes setting product attributes easy	Catalog - Products - Attributes
Banner Ad in a Box	Run advertisements for other sites in an InfoBox	Tools – Banners*
Basic Template Structure 1.3 + Fixes	Make changes to all pages on one template page rather than dozens	Design Control-Template Admin
Category Box Enhancement 1.1	Customizable bullet graphics for category listings	Design Controls – InfoBox Admin
Column Product Listing MS2	Multiple column display for your product pages	Configuration – Maximum Values
Credit Card in a Box	An InfoBox that lists the credit cards you accept	Design Controls – InfoBox Admin*
Credit Class/Gift Voucher/Discount Coupons	Give gift certificates and coupons to customers	Gift Vouchers/Coupons
CCV Credit Card Verify	Capture customer's credit card CCV number for better security against fraud.	Modules - Payments
Define Mainpage v1.2	Write or edit your home page welcome text as easy as using Word	Info System – Define MainPage
DHTML Menu in Admin	Navigate your admin with half the clicks with this drop-down menu instead of left-column menus	Configuration – Enable DHTML Menu
Donate for non-profit site	An InfoBox to allow customers to donate to you	Design Controls – InfoBox Admin*
Down for Maintenance v1.1b	Stop purchases and customize the display during site maintenance, while keeping the site available.	Configuration – Site Maintenance
Download_Controller v5.3 MS2.2	Complete control over download purchases. Set how many downloads are allowed and when they expire.	Configuration – Downloads*
Easy Populate Advanced 2.75 with Froogle Support	Easily edit and update your database using Excel, then upload any number of products. Upload to FROOGLE to	Catalog – EasyPopulate*

	increase sales	
Edit Orders 1.56 MS2	Enter orders and customers for orders received from phone or other non-web source	**Customers/Orders – Create New Order or Create New Customer**
EFSnet Payment Module	Extra payment module to use EFS.net for credit card processing	**Modules – Payments**
FAQ Desk 1.01	Create or update FAQ's as easy as using Word	**FAQ Desk**
FedX 1.11 MS2	Extra shipping module to use FedEx for shipping	**Modules – Payments**
GeoTrust/SkipJack Payment Module	Extra payment module to use GetTrust or SkipJack for credit card processing	**Modules – Payments**
Google Ads InfoBox	Display ads by Google and make money if your customers click it	**Banner Manager and Design Controls – InfoBox Admin**
Infobox Admin v1.1MS2	Easily add pages to your Information Infobox	Design Controls – InfoBox Admin
Level Discount	Give price breaks when customers order over a certain amount of dollars or items	**Modules - Order Total - Price Break Discount**
Meta Tag Controller/ Generator	Assigns meta tags to each product on Products page	**Catalog - Products**
MonthlySales&Tax1.55	A sales tax report that extracts the information your accountant needs to do your tax reports	**Reports – Monthly Sales/Tax**
Mysql Backup	Backs up even the largest database with ease	**Tools - Backup**
News Desk 1.48.3	Create or update news articles as easy as using Word	**NewsDesk**
OSC-Affiliate 1.09	A powerful affiliate program to let others sell your product for you, you pay commissions	**Affilates**
osC-PrintOrder w/logo v1.0	Print store orders that display your store logo	**No Admin settings**
PayBox Payment Module	Extra payment module to use PayBox for payments	**Modules - Payment**
PayJunction	One-stop, full-service for US vendors to accept payments from customers worldwide.	**Modules - Payment**
Pay Me Now	Credit Card processor for U.S. vendors with U.S. banks.	**Modules - Payment**
Paypal Shopping Cart IPN 2.8 NEW!	Notifies your database that a payment has been completed; now *automatically installed* when you specify PayPal (must also set up on PayPal site)	**Modules - Payment**
Purchase w/o Account	Customers no longer have to register	**Configuration –**

	to buy	Purchase w/o Acct
Quantity Discount	Discount based on the number of items in the cart	**Modules - Order Total - Price Break Discount**
SaleMaker 2.2MS2v1.01	Easily set sales on products, percent or flat pricing	**Catalog - SaleMaker**
Shop by Price	InfoBox that allows customers to view all items sorted by price ranges you specify	**Catalog - Shop By Price**
Specials On Main Page	Specials InfoBox on main page	**Design Controls – Template Mgmt.**
Super-Friendly Admin Menu NEW!	All links on main Administration Menu	**No Admin settings**
Template Install & Config. V1.2	Easily configures templates to look the way you want	**Design Controls – Template Mgmt.**
Ultra Pics NEW!	Multiple views of products	**Catalog - Products**
UPS Choice 1.8	Allows customers to specify UPS shipping methods	**Modules - Shipping**
USPS Methods 2.5	Allows customers to specify USPS shipping methods	**Modules - Shipping**
Who's Online InfoBox	InfoBox of how many customers in your store now.	**Design Controls – InfoBox Admin - Who's Online**
Wish list V 2.2	Allows customers to add products to wish list	**Design Controls – InfoBox Admin – Wish List**
WYSIWYG HTML Editor for Admin 1.7	Generate text on many stock osCommerce pages as easy as using Word	**Automatic; change in Configuration – WYSIWYG Editor 1.7**
Cross Sell X-Sell MS2	Suggest related products to sell more per customer.	**Catalog – X-Sell***

*Additional setup is required. See item detail.

Chapter

3

How to *Set Up* Your Store Using CRE Loaded 6.1 Version of osCommerce

In this chapter:

This chapter contains user instructions on how to set up the several dozen features of CRE Loaded osCommerce. They are grouped for easy reference by their menu item in CRE 6.1's main Admin Menu. This chapter covers only the features in the Store Setup column.

Level of difficulty: It's a breeze! Practically sets itself up for you *and* cooks you breakfast.

The main Administrative Menu of CRE Loaded OSC 6.1 is divided into two columns: Store Management and Store Setup.

Store Management: the LEFT COLUMN – items you will use on a daily basis, and

Store Setup: the RIGHT COLUMN - items you will probably use the first time, then only occasionally thereafter.

In this chapter we review the *right column Store Setup* section and examine each feature that is unique to CRE Loaded OSC 6.1. Refer back to p. 12.

a. Configuration Setup Menu

Most contributions have additional settings in this configuration menu. This chapter includes *only those whose MAIN SETTINGS in this menu.* **Downloads Controller, Stock, WYSIWYG Editor,** and **Site Maintenance** are features covered in this section.

My Store – Enable DHTML Menu

The My Store menu in CRE Loaded 6.15 and above contains an extra setting that allow you to navigate your admin with half the clicks of the left-hand menu with a top navigation bar with drop-down menus instead of the left-column menus.

To use the DHTML Menu, from the main **Administration** Menu on p. 12, select **CONFIGURATION – My Store - Enable DHTML Menu.**

Change the setting to TRUE to show the drop-down Admin menus, or FALSE to remove them.

Click the **UPDATE Button.**

Minimum Values

While most settings in this menu are the same as in osCommerce, there are three that concern us here: Best Sellers, Also Purchased, and Cross Sell. If you turn these InfoBoxes off in other menus, you must remember to change their minimum values in this menu to ZERO. If you turn them on, they will display the default of one item until you change their value here.

Minimum Values

Title	Value	Action
Best Sellers	1	ⓘ
Also Purchased	1	ⓘ
X-Sell	1	ⓘ

Stock Control

You can use your store as an inventory management and control program with this powerful module. Each time a customer makes a purchase, your stock level will tick down by one item. It can warn you when your stock hits the pre-set re-order level.

To use the Inventory Management program, from the main **Administration Menu on page 12**, select **CONFIGURATION – STOCK**.

This brings you to the **Stock Configuration** menu. Click the **EDIT button** to edit each of the settings, as follows:

Stock

Title	Value	Action
Check stock level	false	ⓘ
Subtract stock	false	ⓘ
Allow Checkout	true	ⓘ
Mark product out of stock	***	ⓘ
Stock Re-order level	5	▶

Set to true if you wish to use this module. It will then check if stock is available before allowing purchase

Subtract product from stock total

Allow checkout even if stock is insufficient

What to display when stock is below re-order level

Define when stock needs to be re-ordered

Download/Downloads Controller

If you will be selling a product to be downloaded upon checkout such as an Ebook or software, this feature of CRE Loaded osCommerce makes it easy.

NOTE: Directions for this feature are different from standard osCommerce: setup is much more automatic and requires little or no programming.

Download Controller Action Summary:	Administrative Module:
1. Set download configuration	Configuration - Download
2. Set Product Attribute as "Download"	Catalog – Products – select product and select Download attribute.
3. Upload the product to be downloaded	Tools – File Manager or use your FTP Client
4. Set permissions on directories the controller needs to read	Use your FTP Client and follow instructions below

1. Set Download Configuration:

From the main Administration menu on p. 12, select CONFIGURATION – DOWNLOAD. This brings you to the Download Configuration menu:

Downloads

Title	Value
Enable download	true
Download by redirect	false
Expiry delay (days)	7
Maximum number of downloads	1
Downloads Controller Update Status Value	4
Downloads Controller Download on hold message	 <font color="FF0000">NOTE: Downloads are not available until payment has been confirmed</font>
Downloads Controller Order Status Value	2

Set to true to enable downloads after checkout. If you wish to use browser redirection for download. Disable on non-Unix systems.

Number of days before the download link expires. 0 means unlimited.

Total number of downloads authorized before customer link expires.

Which orders_status resets the Download days and Max Downloads - Default is 4

What message to display when Download is on on hold i.e. pending confirmation of payment

Downloads Controller Download on hold message

Downloads Controller Order Status Value - Default=2

2. Set Product Attribute as "Download":

Using the **Administrative Module**, go to **Administration, Catalog, Products.** If you have previously enabled download correctly in Step 1, you will see a box below the "Product Attributes" section where you can add the product as a download.

3. Upload the product:

From the main **Administrative Menu**, go to Tools – File Manager. Select the file name of your product download and click the UPLOAD button. OR use your FTP program to **u**pload the product to be downloaded into the store's download folder:

/<u>download</u>/

4. Set permissions on directories the controller needs to read:

The download status will be read from the folder store/**pub**/, therefore, you or your installer need to change the permissions on that directory: Use your FTP Client to select CHMOD and change permissions for the /pub/ directory to 777 and /download/ to 755.

WYSIWYG Editor 1.7 Configuration

This defines where the WYSIWYG (or HTML or Word-like) Editor is available so you do not have to manually code the text on your pages. There is no need for you to alter these settings unless you have a reason for changing them.

WYSIWYG Editor 1.7

Title	Value	Action
PRODUCT DESCRIPTIONS use WYSIWYG HTMLAREA?	Enable	►
PRODUCT DESCRIPTIONS use JPSY-PHP ULTRA-IMAGES MANAGER?	Enable	ⓘ
Product Description Basic/Advanced Version?	Advanced	ⓘ
Product Description Layout Width	505	ⓘ
Product Description Layout Height	240	ⓘ
CUSTOMER EMAILS use WYSIWYG HTMLAREA?	Enable	ⓘ
Customer Email Basic/Advanced Version?	Advanced	ⓘ
Customer Email Layout Width	505	ⓘ
Customer Email Layout Height	240	ⓘ

Product Descriptions:

Enable editor
Enable images
Enables more or fewer text buttons (bold, color, etc.)

Width of editing window
Height of editing window

Customer Emails:
Enable editor
Enables more or fewer text buttons (bold, color, etc.)
Width of editing window
Height of editing window

NEWSLETTER EMAILS use WYSIWYG HTMLAREA?	Enable	ⓘ	**Newsletter Emails:** Enable editor
Newsletter Email Basic/Advanced Version?	Advanced	ⓘ	Enables more or fewer text buttons (bold, color, etc.)
Newsletter Email Layout Width	505	ⓘ	Width of editing window
Newsletter Email Layout Height	240	ⓘ	Height of editing window
DEFINE MAINPAGE use WYSIWYG HTMLAREA?	Enable	ⓘ	**MAIN PAGE Text:** Enable editor
Define Mainpage Basic/Advanced Version?	Advanced	ⓘ	Enables more or fewer text buttons (bold, color, etc.)
Define Mainpage Layout Width	605	ⓘ	Width of editing window
Define Mainpage Layout Height	300	ⓘ	Height of editing window
GLOBAL - User Interface Font Type	Times New Roman	ⓘ	**GLOBAL EDITING SETTINGS:**
GLOBAL - User Interface Font Size	12	ⓘ	Font type
GLOBAL - User Interface Font Colour	Black	ⓘ	Font size Font color
GLOBAL - User Interface Background Colour	White	ⓘ	Background View the live-html as you
GLOBAL - ALLOW DEBUG MODE?	0	ⓘ	type in a 2nd field above.

Affiliate Program Configuration

See Affiliate Program section in Chapter 4 for full instructions.

Site Maintenance Configuration

This module allows you to temporarily take down your store while you perform maintenance, preventing aborted or uncompleted transactions during your maintenance and keeping your database intact. It's like putting a sign on the door, "back in 30 minutes." Without it, it's like washing your store floors while customers wander about, slipping and sliding and wondering why they are lying on your floor.

From the main Admin menu shown on p. 12, select **Configuration – Site Maintenance.** This brings you to the **Site Maintenance Configuration** menu.

You can select whether all columns should be hidden during maintenance, or which ones will continue to display, if you wish; or you may simply accept the default settings.

Follow the instructions on the table below to enable **Site Maintenance.**

Site Maintenance

Title	Value	
Down for Maintenance: ON/OFF	false	Set to TRUE to perform maintenance on your website.
Down for Maintenance: filename	down_for_maintenance.php	The name of the file that displays the Down for Maintenance prompt.
Down for Maintenance: Hide Header	false	Choose whether or not to hide your header.
Down for Maintenance: Hide Column Left	true	Choose whether or not to hide your left and right columns, and footer.
Down for Maintenance: Hide Column Right	true	
Down for Maintenance: Hide Footer	false	Choose whether or not to hide your prices during maintenance.
Down for Maintenance: Hide Prices	false	
Down For Maintenance (exclude this IP-Address)	your IP (ADMIN)	Enter your IP address if you wish to continue accessing your catalog during maintenance.
NOTIFY PUBLIC Before going Down for Maintenance: ON/OFF	false	Display a notice on your home page before taking your site down.
Date and hours for notice before maintenance	19/05/2003 between the hou of 11.00-11.30 PM	Set the date and time of the maintenance notice.
Display when webmaster has enabled maintenance	true	Display the notice when you have selected TRUE for the Down for Maintenance module.
Display website maintenance period	false	Set and display the estimated amount of time your site will be down.
Website maintenance period	0h30	

Purchase Without Account

This module allows your customers to purchase without first creating a username and password. While this is very cool and likely results in additional orders, if any of these additional orders has a question about their account they must send an inquiry by email, you must research their problem or question, and email back a personal reply.

From the main Admin menu shown on p. 12, select **Configuration – Purchase Without Account.** This brings you to the **Purchase Without Account** menu.

If you wish to allow customers to purchase without opening an account, set this to TRUE. From the main Admin menu shown on p. 12, select CONFIGURATION – ACCOUNTS. Click the EDIT Button, then change the radio button to TRUE. Click the SAVE Button.

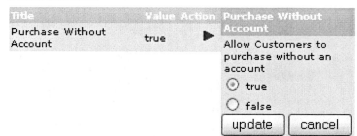

Links Manager

See Links Manager section in Chapter 4 for full instructions.

b. Modules – Payment

While many of the menu items in the Payment menu are the same in osCommerce and CRE Loaded, several are new. New items include:

Credit Card with CCV Verification Checking:

Adds an extra box to the manual Credit Card processing module so you can receive the 3-digit code from the back of the customer's card, and reduce fraud. The Credit Card module is for retailers who manually process credit cards - for example, retailers who already have a credit card machine or other way of processing cards.

To use the Credit Card with CCV program, from the main Administration Menu, select MODULES - Payment - Credit Card with CCV. If you wish to add CCV checking and your credit card processor supports it, change the item ENABLE CCV CODE to TRUE:

Enable CCV code
Do you want to enable ccv code checking?

⊙ True
○ False

For security reasons, only part of the customer's credit card number will be emailed to you. The rest will be found in the customer's record when you review and edit your orders.

Remember, if you enable CCV checking you MUST enter your email address so it can be emailed to you.

PayJunction

This is a one-stop, full-service credit card processor for U.S. vendors with U.S. banks, accepts credit cards from customers world-wide. They even have a free analysis service to lower the rates for businesses that already have merchant accounts. Easy setup, excellent customer service, and no resellers to go through. Only $15 a month, 2.2% + thirty cents per transaction. There is a one-time fee of $350; most store owners with good sales volume will find Pay Junction cheaper in the long run because of the very low monthly and transaction fees. Low-volume store owners will not benefit.

To use PayJunction as your payment processor, you must first register with PayJunction: **Contact their Sales Manager for fastest service: mfrancl@payjunction.com**

To set up your store to accept PayJunction, once you have received your account name from PayJunction, from the main Administration Menu, select **MODULES - PAYMENT** and select **PayJunction**. This brings you to the **PayJunction** menu. Click the EDIT button to edit each of the settings, as follows:

Credit Card : PayJunction

Enable PayJunction Module
Do you want to accept PayJunction payments?

◉ True

○ False

Must be set to TRUE to accept payments through PayJunction.

Enter the username the sales manager gave you.

username
The username for your PayJunction service

`commerce`

Prompt for CVV2/CVC2 code?
Prompt for CVV2/CVC2 code for additional security.

○ Yes

◉ No

If you want "Credit Card verification" fraud checking and have paid for this additional service, select YES. Otherwise, select NO. To add on Pay Junction CCV2 checking, click here.

Only test transactions?
Run only test transactions.

◉ Yes

○ No

Leave this at YES while you do test transactions so the credit card accounts you use during testing will NOT be charged. But be CERTAIN to change to "NO" when you are ready for real customers, or your real customers will not be charged, either!

Payment Zone

If a zone is selected, only enable this payment module for that zone.

--none--

Set Order Status

Set the status of orders made with this payment module to this value

default

Sort order of display.

Sort order of display. Lowest is displayed first.

0

update   cancel

If you only wish to accept this payment method for a certain zone, for example locally or only in a certain country, enter that zone here. You must have previously set up the zones in Localization/Zones.

Leave Order Status at "default" unless you have a reason to change. For example, if you pre-authorize sales you may wish to change the status to "Pending" until it is actually processed. If you leave the sort order at 0, it will not display to your customers. Any other number will determine what order it displays on your payment page compared to the other payment modules you have activated.

When you have finished, click the UPDATE Button.

Modules – Shipping:

While many of the menu items in the Shipping menu are the same in osCommerce and CRE Loaded, one very useful module is new, Zones World.

Zones World 2.0:

New shipping module allows you to set flat shipping rates based on up to 3 zones of your choice. For example, state, country, and international. To use the Zones World program, from the main Administration Menu, select MODULES - SHIPPING and click ZONES:

This brings you to the Zones World menu. Click the EDIT button to edit each of the settings, as follows:

World Zone Rates

Enable Zones Method
Do you want to offer zone rate shipping?

○ True
○ False

Tax Class
Use the following tax class on the shipping fee.

[--none-- ▾]

Sort Order
Sort order of display.

[0]

Zone 1 Countries
Comma separated list of two character ISO country codes that are part of Zone 1.

[NL]

Zone 1 Shipping Table
Shipping rates to Zone 1 destinations based on a group of maximum order weights. Example: 3:8.50,7:10.50,... Weights less than or equal to 3 would cost 8.50 for Zone 1 destinations.

[5:5.00,7:10.00,99:100.]

Zone 1 Handling Fee
Handling Fee for this shipping zone

[0]

Must be set to TRUE for this module to work.

Are you required to charge tax on shipping? Check with your tax expert to be sure.

If you offer multiple shipping choices, do you want this to be displayed first, second or what in relation to the other shipping methods?

Enter the country code or codes from LOCALIZATION - COUNTRIES for your closest zone, Zone 1. If more than 1, put a comma between each one BUT no spaces (see example in Zone 2 Countries next). Enter the rates for that zone based on weight. In the example, up to a 5 lb (or kg, it is indifferent to the actual units) package would cost $5.00 in shipping. From 5.01 to 7 lbs/kg, the shipping charged would be $10. From 7.01 to 99 lbs/kg, the shipping is $100. Be sure to remove all these old codes to avoid surprising your customers with a $100 shipping fee!

If you wish to add a separate handling fee to cover packaging, labels, etc. enter it here.
REPEAT these 4 boxes (Counties, Shipping Table, & Handling Fees) for Zone 2 and 3.

In Zone 3 you may optionally enter "All Others" (without the quotes) rather than every country code!

Click the **UPDATE Button** when finished.

Modules – Order Total

Level or Price Break Discount:

Price Break Discount in allows you to give price breaks when customers order over a certain amount. You will wish to mention this discount somewhere in your site, and/or in an email that you send to your loyal customers.

To use the Level Discount program, from the main Administration Menu shown on p. 12, select **Modules - Order Total - Price Break Discount.**

Everything is self-explanatory except for the item DISCOUNT PERCENTAGE:

Discount Percentage
Set the price breaks and discount percentages
`100:7.5,250:10,500:12`

How much of a price break do you want to offer? This example shows
A 7.5% discount if the order is $100 or more
A 10% discount if the order is over $250; and
a 12% discount if the order is over $500.

Quantity Discount:

Quantity-specific discount based on the number of items in the cart. May be a flat rate (i.e. buy 5 get $5 off) or Percentage (i.e. buy 4 items get 20% off). To use the **Quantity Discount** program, from the main Administration Menu, select **Modules - Order Total - Global Quantity Discount.** : This brings you to the **Global Quantity Discount** menu. Click the EDIT button to edit each of the settings. All are self-explanatory and/or include detailed instructions on the menu.

c. Administrator Menu

Admin Access Levels

This feature allows you to easily secure your store with password protection. It also allows you to set access for different employees to different parts of your store. For example, you may have an employee who needs to process orders, but not get into the payment setup sections. It contains a password forgotten module which will send a new password to your registered email address, and will issue new passwords to new employees.

Login Panel:

E-Mail Address: [   ]

Password: [   ]

[confirm]

Password forgotten?

Admin Access Action Summary:	Administrative Module:
1. Insert your own name as the top administrator	Administrator – Member Groups
2. Add accounts for other employees who need it. They will receive NEW ADMIN ACCOUNT email with temporary password.	Administrator – Member Groups – New Member
3. Set or Hide the modules that will be visible (and accessible to members) in the Admin Module	Administrator – File Access

1. Insert your own name as the Top Administrator:

The **FIRST** thing you do when you get your new CRE-Loaded store is to ***insert your own name*** in the TOP ADMINISTRATOR account.

From the main Administrative menu, go to Administrator – Member Groups and click **EDIT button.** Enter **your own name** and click the **INSERT button.**

If you LOSE your password and haven't put *your name* in as the top administrator, or your email address has changed since you set it, you will NOT be able to use the "LOST PASSWORD" feature. It's like a padlock that can never be opened.
TIP: Set *two* access accounts for yourself so that if you ever change email addresses, you will still be able to access your Administration Module using the other email account.

TIP: You will receive a system email at the email address you specify, telling you that the email address was changed.

2. Set Administrative Access:

Now you can begin setting access for others. To begin setting access, from the main **Administrative Menu shown on p. 12,** select **Administrator – Member Groups:**

This brings up the **Admin Members** menu:

Admin Members

Name	Email Address	Groups Level	LogNum	Action
Master Admin	you@youraddress.com	Top Administrator	28	▶

Displaying **1** to **1** (of **1** members)   [groups]   [new member]
Page 1 of 1

To edit your own email address, click the **EDIT button** (to the right of this menu - not shown above). To add new **groups,** read below.

TIP: You must *first* create the groups, then add the new members to them.

Admin Groups

This is where you create or modify groups and the access privileges the group will have. For example, the top administrator has access to all areas of the Admin. You can create a separate group called "Order Processors" who are only permitted to access the Catalog section so they can fulfill orders.

To create a group, click the **GROUPS button.** This brings you to the **ADMIN GROUPS screen:**

To add a **NEW GROUP**, click the **NEW GROUP button**, give the group a name such as "Order Processors" and click the **SAVE button**.

To expand the access privileges or permissions of an existing group, highlight it and click the **NEW PERMISSION button.**

To **edit the NAME** of a group, click the **EDIT button.**

To **delete a group**, click the **DELETE button.**

To add new members to an admin group, return to the **Admin Members menu** and select the **NEW MEMBERS button.** A temporary password will be emailed by the system to the new member, along with a link to the site.

4. Set or Hide the modules that will be visible in the Admin Module

This menu removes items from the Administrative Module. Be careful if you decide to use it! Unless you know you will never, ever need to use a module, why not simply leave this menu alone?

Admin "Boxes" Menu

 CAUTION: If you must remove a module from your Admin, first store a backup copy of the associated files. If you uninstall one of the InfoBoxes from this menu, all files stored in that module are also permanently removed!

Step 1. Make a copy of the files.

Select the box by clicking the Action button, then click **STORE FILES.** This takes you to the **Admin Boxes STORE FILES Menu.**

Step 2. Disable access to the module:

From the main Admin Boxes menu, click the **Red button** to disable an item from the Administrative Module. **THE CONTENTS IS GONE FOREVER!**

c. Design Controls Menu

Template Admin

Wow, this is the most radical and profound difference between standard osCommerce and osCommerce CRE Loaded. And what a difference it is! No more editing DOZENS of pages to change the look of your site – simply go to the DESIGN CONTROL menu and make a few clicks, and they are IMMEDIATELY applied throughout your site!

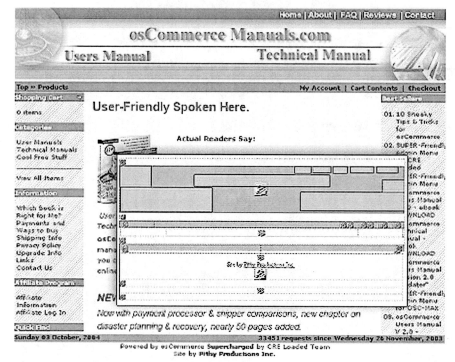

A main page template and the page it creates.

NOTE: If you are accustomed to using standard osCommerce, learning BTS will take some getting used to. You used to edit the files in includes/languages/ english/filename.php/ Well, with BTS you can edit those files all you want – it won't do a thing, your edits will simply not appear in your catalog. Doh! But once you get accustomed to going to the templates directory to make your changes, then you will never want to use a non-templated site again.

Here are the changes that can now be performed in the Administrative Module using the Templates Admin menu instead of php programming:

General:
Set site width

Header:
Include cart in header
Languages in header
Header Link Buttons

Body:
Main table cellpadding
Sub table cellpadding
Left column include or exclude
Right column include or exclude

Infoboxes middle column:
Deault specials
example.html
featured.php
mainpage.php
new_products.php
newsdesk.php
newsdesk_sticky.php
upcoming products.php

Other:
Show customer greeting
Border around main page
Mainpage headers

Template Action Summary	Administrative Module:
1. Change Templates	DESIGN CONTROLS – TEMPLATE ADMIN – click Action column of template wanted – click SET TO DEFAULT.
2. Add or Remove left or right column	DESIGN CONTROLS – TEMPLATE ADMIN – Edit – Include Left or Right Column
3. Set contents of middle column (mainpage)	DESIGN CONTROLS – TEMPLATE ADMIN – Edit – Select Modules for Main Page
4. Add or remove InfoBoxes from left or right column	DESIGN CONTROLS – INFOBOX ADMIN – click green button to add, red to remove.
5. Move position of InfoBoxes up or down	DESIGN CONTROLS – Infobox Admin – click red arrow to move infobox up; gold arrow to move it down.
6. Add or remove links or pages that display in Information InfoBox	INFO SYSTEM – INFO MANAGER. See Info System section.

7. Edit text or images that displays on ALL pages: HEADER & FOOTER	templates/main_page.tpl.php
8. Change look of ALL InfoBoxes	templates/ box.tpl.php
9. Change buttons used in templates	templates/(templatename)/images/buttons
10. Change LOGO.GIF	templates/(templatename)/images/logo.gif

TIP: If it's on ALL pages, you probably edit it in the template. If it's only on ONE or A FEW pages, it remains in includes/languages/english/ directory.

To create your own CUSTOM TEMPLATE, first select the template closest to the look you want to achieve and modify it.

To Select or Edit a Template

To select a template for your website, from the main Administrative Menu on p. 12, go to **DESIGN CONTROL – TEMPLATE ADMIN.** This brings you to the **TEMPLATE MANAGEMENT menu:**

Template Management

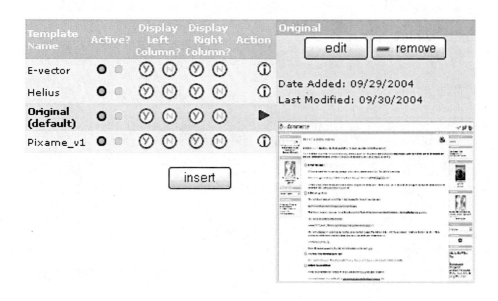

To Change Your Website's Template

Four templates are pre-loaded for you in CRE-LOADED, including the classic Original (look of standard osCommerce). An example of each follows; see the **TEMPLATE NAME on each sample under the "What's New Here?" greeting.**

To change the look of your entire website with just one click, highlight that template name in the **ACTION** column, click the **EDIT** button, and the **EDIT TEMPLATE** menu comes up. Check the **SET AS DEFAULT button** as show below, then click the **SAVE BUTTON** at the bottom of the page:

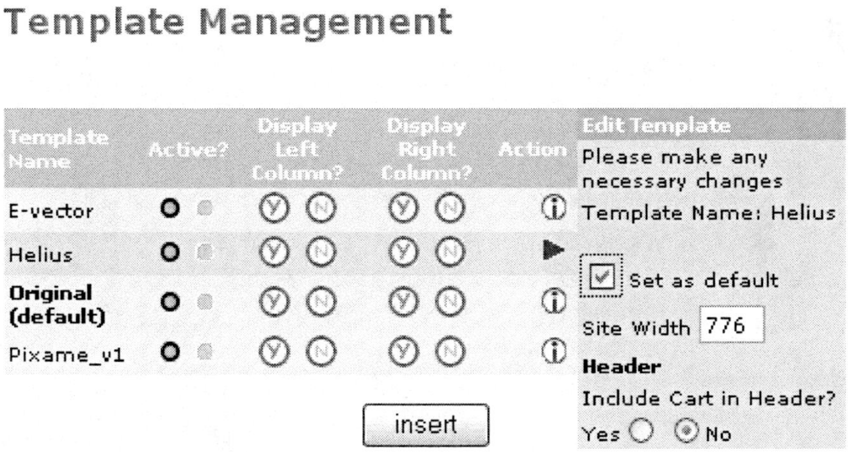

Template Management

Template Name	Active?	Display Left Column?	Display Right Column?	Action	Edit Template
					Please make any necessary changes
E-vector	O ○	Ⓨ Ⓝ	Ⓨ Ⓝ	ⓘ	Template Name: Helius
Helius	O ○	Ⓨ Ⓝ	Ⓨ Ⓝ	▶	
Original (default)	O ○	Ⓨ Ⓝ	Ⓨ Ⓝ	ⓘ	☑ Set as default
Pixame_v1	O ○	Ⓨ Ⓝ	Ⓨ Ⓝ	ⓘ	Site Width 776

insert

Header

Include Cart in Header?

Yes ○ ◉ No

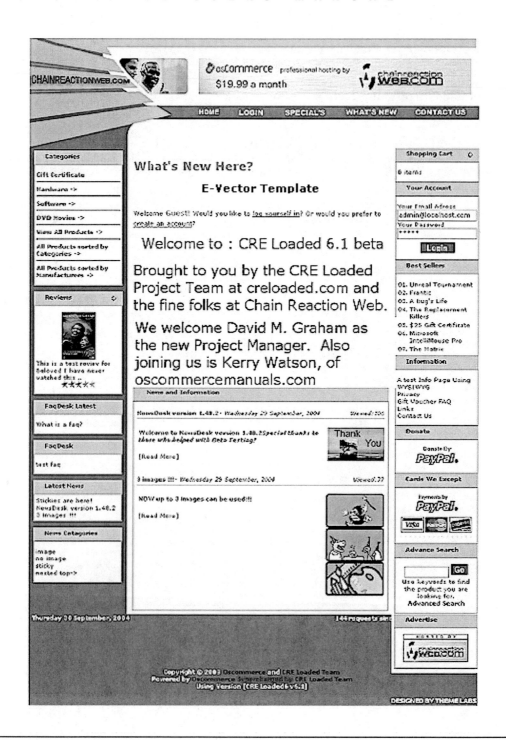

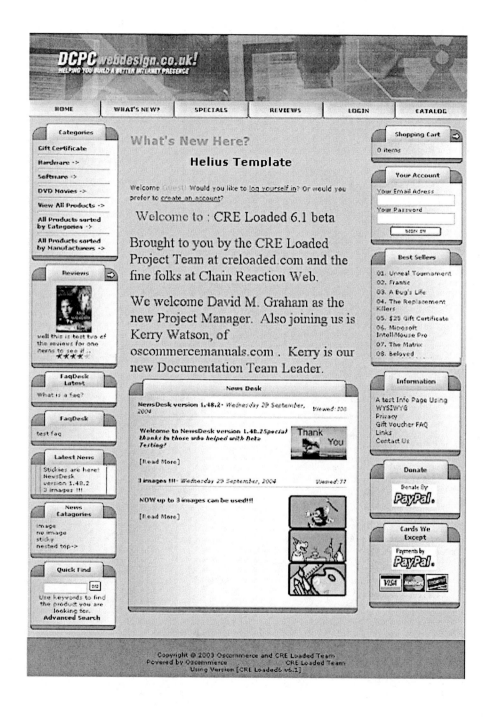

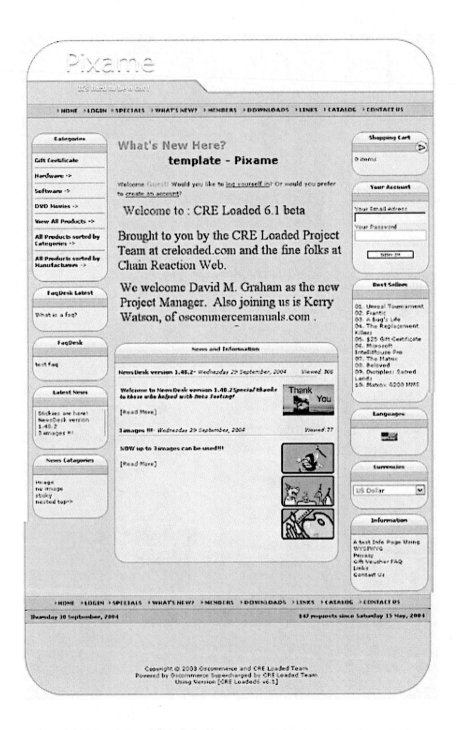

To Make Changes to Your Website's Template

Edit Template

Please make any necessary changes
Template Name: Original

Site Width `750`

Header
Include Cart in Header?
Yes ○   ⊙ No

Include languages in Header?
Yes ○   ⊙ No

Include Header Link Buttons?
Yes ⊙   ○ No

Table cellpadding
Main table cellpadding `3` ▾

Sub table cellpadding `8` ▾

Side infobox cellpadding
Left side cellpadding `1` ▾

Right side cellpadding `1` ▾

Left column
Include the left column?
Yes ⊙   ○ No

Left column width (pixel) `130`

Left column cellpadding `3` ▾

Right column
Include the right column?
Yes ⊙   ○ No

Right column width (pixel) `130`

Right column cellpadding `3` ▾

You may set width on Original to 750 (default) OR to 100% but watch header width if you use a percentage.

Show or hide cart in header

Show or hide languages in header

Show or hide header link buttons:

Add or remove padding in each table

Add or remove padding in each sub-table

Add or remove padding in each left infobox

Add or remove padding in each right infobox

Include or remove the left column

Set left column width

Set left column padding

Include or remove the right column

Set right column width

Set right column padding

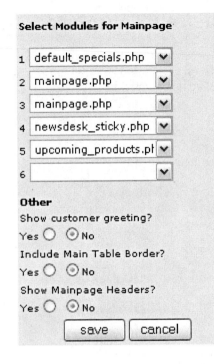

Main Page Modules: **SEE EXAMPLES BELOW**

Set which boxes will display in the MAIN PAGE.

Set the order in which they display by selecting the top box first, second box next, and so forth.

To skip one or all features, leave the box blank.

NOTE: These other items only apply to templates that include the following features:

Show the "What's New Here?" greeting

Include or hide a border around the main table

Show or hide header

Click **SAVE button** to save your changes.

Main Page Module Selections

See samples of each infobox following this table:

Default Specials Infobox
Example Infobox
Featured Products Infobox
Main Page Text (Welcome text)
New Products Infobox
News Desk Infobox
News Desk Stickies Infobox
Upcoming Products Infobox

Sample Default Specials, New Products, & Upcoming Products:

| $25 Gift Certificate $25.00 | Hewlett Packard LaserJet 1100Xi $499.99 | Microsoft IntelliMouse Explorer $64.95 |

Example.html:

Welcome Guest! Would you like to log yourself in? Or would you prefer to create an account?

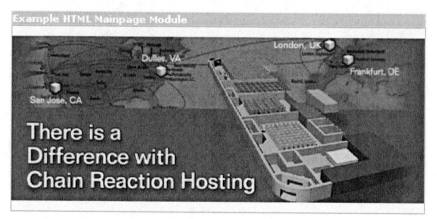

News Desk:

News and Information

NewsDesk version 1.48.2- *Wednesday 29 September, 2004*   *Viewed: 108*

Welcome to NewsDesk version 1.48.2*Special thanks to those who helped with Beta Testing!*

[Read More]

3 images !!!- *Wednesday 29 September, 2004*   *Viewed: 77*

NOW up to 3 images can be used!!!

[Read More]

News Desk Stickies:

News Desk Stickies

Stickies are here!- *Wednesday 29 September, 2004*   *Viewed: 60*

Welcome to the Sticky area

Stickies have been implemented in v1.48.2

Is this not a nifty feature?

[Read More]

Stickies are here

Other Changes to Template – Custom Templates

Many more changes can be made to the template. You can always change it back if you don't like it!

To easily make your own CUSTOM TEMPLATE, simply:
1. Select the template that is closest to the look you want.
2. GET a copy of the images in the template.
3. REPLACE THEM with your own custom images with the same name.
4. Make changes to the template file and CSS file until you are satisfied.

InfoBox Administration Menu

This powerful and important menu controls the display of EVERY BOX in the left and right columns, including whether they are displayed or not, their position, and whether they are in the left or right column. You can also change the looks (font, color) in this menu.

SOME boxes are totally controlled by this menu, while others have additional settings.

Infobox Display, Create & Update

Title	Activate Box?	Set Column	Position	Action
Donate	⦿ ○	⇦ ⇨	⬆ ⬇	ⓘ
Cards We Accept	⦿ ○	⇦ ⇨	⬆ ⬇	ⓘ
Advance Search	○ ⦿	⇦ ⇨	⬆ ⬇	ⓘ
Wishlist	⦿ ○	⇦ ⇨	⬆ ⬇	ⓘ

To use the **InfoBox Admin menu,** from the main **Administration menu** shown on p. 12, select **DESIGN CONTROLS – Infobox Admin.** This brings you to the above menu (which has been edited to fit onto this page). A list of boxes controlled by this menu in 6.15 are shown here, with other settings that are required, if any:

InfoBox	**What it Does:**
Advertise	An infobox where you can display ads for other sites. Must also add banners in TOOLS – BANNER MANAGER.
Affiliate Info	Set up in Affiliate Program
Best Sellers	Best Sellers calculated by the program
Cards We Accept	List of credit cards you accept, must manually edit images or file includes/boxes/card1.php
Categories - 5 different views	Click each one to see which you prefer.
Currencies	Display the currencies you have specified in Localization-Currencies.

Donate	Lets the donor specify any amount they wish to donate via PayPal, must manually edit includes/boxes/donate.php
FAQ Desk	From FAQ Desk.
Featured	Must also be set in Design Controls – Template Admin.
Gift Voucher	Set up in Gift Vouchers.
Google Ad	Display ads by Google and make money if your customers click it.
Information	See Info System menu for setup info.
Languages	Display the Languages you have specified in Localization-Languages.
Links	See Links menu.
Manufacturers	See Manufacturers menu.
Manufacturers Info	See Manufacturers menu.
News Desk	See NewsDesk menu.
Notifications	If customers would like to be notified when the product is updated changes.
Order History	After customer has logged on, they can see their history in a box.
Products Latest	Newest products you specified in Design Controls – Template Admin also displayed in a side InfoBox.
Quick Find	Quick Search.
Reviews	Let customers see reviews by others, and write their own reviews.
Search Advanced	Advanced Search.
Select Template	Let customers select their own template during their shopping experience.
Shop by Price	Set price ranges customers can shop in Catalog – Shop by Price.
Shopping Cart	Extra box for shopping cart.
Specials	Extra box for specials.
Tell a Friend	Let guests tell a friend about a product.
Whos Online	Let guests see how many other customers are currently online.
Wishlist	Let guests add products to their own wish list.
You Have a Download	Inform customers who have logged on when their download is ready.
Your Account	A shortcut box for customers who have logged on so they can get to their account more quickly.

e. Info System

This section covers how to create or edit additional pages linked from the **Information InfoBox,** and edit the home page using **Define MainPage. Do not confuse this with the InfoBOX Administration.**

Info Manager

The **Information Manager** makes it a breeze to add, edit, or remove pages in your **INFORMATION INFOBOX.** It's now as easy as typing an email.

From the main Administrative Menu shown on p. 12, select **INFO SYSTEM – INFO MANAGER.** This brings you to the **Information Manager Menu.**

Information

A test Info Page Using WYSIWYG
Privacy
Gift Voucher FAQ
Links
Contact Us

Information Manager

No	A↓ Z	Title	ID	Public	Action
1	1	Which Book is Right for Me?	6	O ○	🖊 🗑
2	2	Payments and Ways to Buy	1	O ○	🖊 🗑
3	3	Shipping Info	2	O ○	🖊 🗑
4	4	Privacy Policy	3	O ○	🖊 🗑
5	5	Upgrade Info	7	O ○	🖊 🗑
6	6	Links	8	O ○	🖊 🗑

new   cancel

To make a page VISIBLE to the public, click the **GREEN** O**button.**
To HIDE a page but keep it on your website, click the **RED** O **button.**

To EDIT your Shipping Information, Privacy Policy, etc. simply click the 🖊.

To DELETE a page, click the 🗑.

Adding New Pages to the Information Manager:
To ADD a new page, click the **NEW button.**
This will bring you to the **ADD INFORMATION TO QUEUE Menu:**

Add information to queue #4

Queue List: 1, 2, 3,

Queue 4 Visible⦿ ☐ (To Do visible)

Title

Description

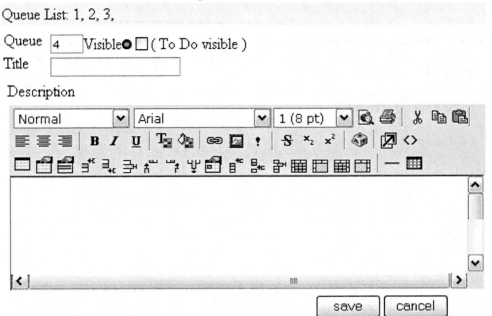

1. QUEUE: The first item in the Information Infobox is 1, second is 2, etc. – think of it as the Sort Order.

2. VISIBLE/INVISIBLE: Click to allow the public to see or hide it if you're not ready to show it yet.

3. TITLE: The link words that the public sees: Contact Us, Shipping Policy, etc.

4. DESCRIPTION: Type the text the public will see on your page. If you are unsure of what a button does, simply hold your cursor over it for a quick explanation.

5. Click SAVE to save your new file.

Define MainPage

Define MainPage allows you to edit your home page text as easily as typing an email.

NOTE: Define MainPage was originally developed for, and can currently be used ONLY in **Internet Explorer**. This will be expanded in future editions.

To begin editing the welcome text on your main page, from the main **Administrative Menu's Catalog** category, and select **DEFINE MAINPAGE**:

This takes you to the **Define MainPage screen shown above**. The default main page displays in the edit box; simply type what you want.

When you are finished, select the **SAVE button** and immediately check your website.

TIP: Hold your cursor over any button in the Define MainPage menu if you are not sure what it is.

If you hate using an editor because it inserts too much code for your advanced techie tastes, click the < > button to toggle between CODE view and WYSIWYG view. Best of both worlds!

f. PayPal IPN Setup Menu

The PayPal menu has been substantially changed since previous versions of CRE Loaded. All PayPal payments now *automatically* incorporate PayPal IPN – Instant Payment Notification – to reduce problems osCommerce had with non-notification of orders after payment with PayPal.

NOTE: Previous versions of CRE Loaded were NOT AUTOMATIC – there are dozens of steps to setting up the old PayPal IPN.

To set up PayPal IPN, you will need to do the following two steps:

 TIP: If you need help, click the [HELP] link at the top of the PayPal IPN menu:

> **PayPal**
> **Enable PayPal Module**
> Do you want to accept PayPal
> payments? [Help]

1. Enable PayPal Module in CRE Loaded:

Go to **Modules – Payment – PayPal** and enter the **email address you use with PayPal,** your **PayPal Business ID or the email address where you received payments,** and the **email address, if any, where you want debug email notifications (error messages) to be sent.** There is no need to make any other changes to the menu unless you know it is necessary, as all the default values are pre-filled in for you.

2. Enable PayPal IPN on PayPal Website:

Go to PayPal.com and set up your PayPal profile to accept IPN: PayPal.com – Profile – Instant Payment Notification Preferences in right-hand menu – Edit. Check the box and enter the FULL URL to the file ipn.php (i.e. if you use "catalog" in your path the full URL would be

        http://www.yourdomainname.com/catalog/ipn.php

| unds | Withdraw | History | Resolution Center | Profile |

Instant Payment Notification Preferences

Instant Payment Notification (IPN)

☑ Instant Payment Notification integrates PayPal payment notification and authentication with your website's back-end operations. Check this box to activate Instant Payment Notification, and enter the URL at which you will receive the payment notifications below. This URL should be a URL which you own and at which you receive HTML posts.

http://www.yourdomainname.com/ipn.php

Save

PayPal Profile – IPN Preferences menu

TIP: You may need to ask your installer or web host for the full path.

TIP: If you skip Step 2, then you will simply be using regular PayPal without IPN. *You may experience problems with customer orders not being reported back to your osCommerce store if they take a long time to complete their transaction OR if they forget to click the final "Click Here to Continue" in PayPal, which returns them and their transaction information to your store.*

g. Links Manager Setup Menu

This contribution allows other sites to link directly to you, moving you up higher in search engine results such as GOOGLE, and also providing valuable related information to your visitors. Saves you valuable time exchanging emails with other sites: "hey, do you want to link to me?" "Sure, what's your url?" "Hey, I did it; what's YOUR url?" Etc. Everyone wins. It's important that the sites be relevant to yours; it will not move you up in search engine rankings (or in your customers' esteem) if you link to a hodge-podge of unrelated sites.

You can use this module to establish specific categories in which you will accept other links; approve, edit, or check links of sites that have submitted potential links to you; and contact one or all of your links partners via email.

Links Action Summary:	Administrative Module:
1. Create Links Categories	Links – Link Categories
2. Approve, add, edit or check Links of partner sites	Links – Links menu
3. Send email to one or all Links partners	Links – Links Contact
4. Change default Links configuration	Configuration - Links
5. Enable or disable Links InfoBox to display	DESIGN CONTROLS – Infobox Admin – click GREEN button next to LINKS*.

TIP: If you do not see the Links infobox in the Infobox Admin menu, then you are using a previous version of CRE Loaded 6.0 and have not properly installed all patches for CRE Loaded 6.0. The patches all must be installed for Links to work correctly in earlier versions.

1. Create Links Categories

To set category names for the types of partners from whom you will accept links, from the main Administrative Menu shown on p. 12, select **LINKS MANAGER – LINK CATEGORIES.** This brings you to the **LINK CATEGORIES Menu:**

Link Categories

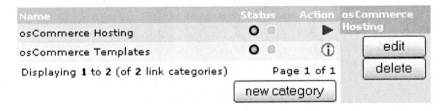

The example above contains two new links categories; osCommerce hosting, and osCommerce Templates.

To ADD another category, select the NEW CATEGORY button and enter the appropriate information as follows:

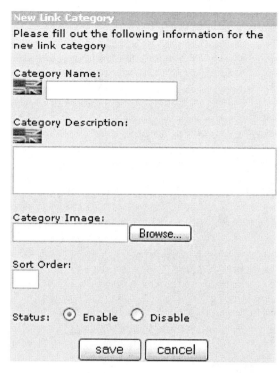

NEW LINKS CATEGORY

Enter a name for the Link Category.

Enter a description of the category to help potential links partners decide if it is right for them. You may include specific details such as "NO ADULT SITES" etc.

Select an image from your computer by clicking BROWSE.

Specify where in the list of other categories this should be: first, second, etc.

Enable or disable the category

Click the **SAVE button** when finished.

Now all you need are some actual Links partners. Send some emails to likely sites encouraging them to submit links. OR if you have their permission, you can add them yourself in the Add Links menu.

2. Approve, add, edit or check Links of partner sites

You should review your links partners periodically to be sure the sites are still there, working properly, haven't morphed into adult sites, etc.

To approve, add, edit or check links of your partner sites, from the main **Admin Menu**'s **LINKS MANAGER menu**, select **LINKS.** This brings you to the **LINKS menu**:

Links

To **approve, edit or check links** of your partner sites, click the appropriate **button** above.

Add New Links

You can add links yourself if you have their permission. To add a link to a partner site yourself, rather than waiting for the other website to get around to it, from the LINKS menu above, click the NEW LINK button.

This brings you to the ADD LINKS page. Simply fill in the appropriate information about the other site and click INSERT.

Add Links
Website Details

Site Title:	_____ * Required
URL:	http:// * Required
Category:	osCommerce Hosting ▾ * Required
Description:	
	Required
Image URL:	http://

Contact

Full Name: [   ] * Required

E-Mail Address: [   ] * Required

Reciprocal Page Details

Reciprocal Page: [http://   ] * Required

Options

Status: [Pending ▾]

Rating: [0   ] * Required

[insert] [cancel]

3. Send email to one or all Links partners

Your links partners are websites that have a special interest in your site. Send them email periodically to keep up the relations, notify them of special news or links-related information such as if your site is moving to a new location.

To send email to one or all Links partners, from the main **Administrative Menu**, select **LINKS MANAGER – Links Contact**. This brings you to the **SEND EMAIL TO LINK PARTNERS page**. Simply fill in the message information and click **SEND EMAIL**:

Link Partner: [Select Link Partner   ▾]

From: [customer.service@oscc]

Subject: [   ]

Message: [   ]

[send mail]

4. Change Default Links Configuration

The standard Links configuration should suit most store owners, but if you are dissatisfied with some feature you will change it here.

To **edit the Links Configuration**, from the main **Administrative Menu**, select **CONFIGURATION – LINKS.** This brings you to the **LINKS CONFIGURATION** page. Change the items you deem necessary to change, as follows:

Links

LINKS CONFIGURATION MENU

Title	Value
Click Count	True
Spider Friendly Links	True
Links Image Width	120
Links Image Height	
Display Link Image	1
Display Link URL	4
Display Link Title	2
Display Link Description	3
Display Link Click Count	5
Link Title Minimum Length	2
Link URL Minimum Length	10
Link Description Minimum Length	10
Link Contact Name Minimum Length	2
Links Check Phrase	

Tracks the number of clicks that you refer to the partner's site.
Makes links search engine-friendly.
Default width of links ads or images.
Default height of links ads or images – leave blank to display actual image height

LINKS SORT ORDER

Numeric order of items displayed;
1=first displayed for each link partner;
2=second item displayed for each link partner, etc.

GLOBAL LINKS CONFIGURATION
Shortest link text you will allow.
Shortest URL you will allow.
Shortest description you will allow.
Shortest contact name.
Phrase the other site MUST contain when you perform a link check or check will fail – should be your company or website name.

5. Enable or Disable Links InfoBox Display

To **enable or disable the display of the Links InfoBox**, from the main **Administration Menu**'s **DESIGN CONTROLS** menu, select **INFOBOX ADMIN.** This brings you to the **Infobox Display, Create and Update Menu.** To **enable Links Infobox**, in the **ACTIVATE Box column**, click the **GREEN button. Also see DESIGN CONTROLS – INFOBOX ADMIN menu if desired.**

h. Other Store Setup Items

These are items that are not specifically linked from a box other than their initial configuration box and/or Design Controls - InfoBox Admin. Most of them require manual editing of files and/or uploading via your FTP Program.

Banner Ad in a Box 1.1

This contribution allows you to display an ad in an InfoBox entitled "Advertise." There are two parts to using this program:

1) Defining the banner ad (specifying the filename, ad size, link, etc.) that you have received from your advertiser, and then
2) Turning the Advertise InfoBox ON.

Step 1.To use the Banner Ad in a Box program, after you have received the ad, link, etc. from your advertiser, from the main Administration Menu, select **TOOLS - BANNER MANAGER.** This brings you to the Banner Manager menu. Click the EDIT button to edit each of the settings, as follows:

Banner Manager

Banner Title:	CRE * Required
Banner URL:	http://www.chainreacti
Banner Group:	box-ad ▾ , or enter a new banner
Image:	[Browse...]

/home/creloaded.com/www/yourstore/
banners/osc-offer.gif

Enter a title for your own reference.
What website do you want the banner to link to?
You must specify "box-ad" for this ad to be used in the box.

Where is the banner ad image on your computer? Browse to find it and Banner Manager will upload it for you.

Image Target
(Save To):   /home/creloaded.com/www/yourstore/

If you want CRE to upload the image, 1) you must have "write" permissions to upload to it and 2) it must end with a "/"

HTML Text:

If you just want a text ad with no image, enter the text here. Banner manager will use the image OR the text, but not both. If you have agreed to start on a certain date, enter it here.

Scheduled At:
(dd/mm/yyyy)

If you have agreed to end the ad on a certain date, enter it here. If you have agreed to give a flat number of viewings or "impressions" of your ad, enter that number INSTEAD of dates. Click the UPDATE Button when you are finished.

Expires On:
(dd/mm/yyyy)   , or at
0   impressions/views.

update   cancel

Step 2. Once your advertiser's "Ad Campaign" has been set up in the above Banner Manager menu, turn the "Advertise" InfoBox on or off in Design Controls - InfoBox Admin. Click the GREEN BUTTON to turn the Advertise InfoBox on. Click the RED BUTTON to turn the Advertise InfoBox off.

TIP: Be sure to test to make sure the ad takes you to the proper place... sometimes an advertiser gives you a link but forgets to put up a page so when your visitors click it they get "Not Found."

Credit Card in a Box

An InfoBox entitled "Cards We Accept" with images of each card that you have selected. This program includes several steps:
1) Selecting the graphic(s) that show which credit cards you accept;
2) (Optional) Linking the PayPal graphic to your PayPal account; and
3) Turning the InfoBox ON.

Step 1. Selecting the Graphics.

There are 21 different images of credit cards in the directory "images/cards/" Find the images of the cards you accept, or create your own.

You may modify the graphic(s) that are displayed two different ways: If you are a beginner, Method A, changing the name of the graphic to match what is already in the program, will be the easiest. If you are an advanced user, Method B, modifying the php file to match the image(s) you want to display, will be easier for you. Neither way is right or wrong.

Changing the Credit Card Graphics, the easy way.

To modify the graphic(s) that shows which card you accept, using your FTP program on your website, navigate to the directory images/cards/.
a. First, save the original images as a backup by changing the name of cards2.gif to cards2-ORIGINAL.gif. In many FTP programs you can do this by highlighting the file cards2.gif and RIGHT-clicking, and from the menu that appears select RENAME.
b. Now change the names of the graphic images that you want, to the names of the graphics in the program, images/cards/cards2.gif AND the PayPal graphic named images/cards/logo-xclick_paypal.gif. Use the same method as in step a.

TIP: To get rid of one image or the other without any programming, simply over-write it by uploading a new 1 pixel transparent gif with the same name.

If you prefer, you can change the names of the images in file includes/boxes/card1.php.

Step 2. Turn the "Credit Cards We Accept" Box ON:

From the main Administration Menu, select Design Controls - InfoBox Admin, then click the Cards We Accept row to highlight it. Click the GREEN BUTTON to turn it ON or the RED BUTTON to turn it off. Click the UP or DOWN ARROW or LEFT or RIGHT arrow to move the box where you want.

TIP: Alternatively, you may also click the EDIT Button at the BOTTOM of the screen, then update the info in the form boxes that appear at the bottom of the page.

Step 3. (OPTIONAL) PayPal Setup
If you wish to have the PayPal image link to your PayPal account, set up your PayPal menu in MODULES - PAYMENTS - PAYPAL.

Donate for Non-Profit Site

An InfoBox entitled "Donate" with a link to PayPal's DONATE program which lets the donor specify any amount they wish to donate. This program includes two parts:
1) **Modifying the link** that takes the donor to your PayPal account and lets them specify the amount; and
2) **Turning the InfoBox ON.**

Step 1. Modify the Link that takes the Visitor to Your PayPal Account

Use your FTP program to "GET" the file includes/boxes/donate.php and SEARCH for the phrase   **donations@creloaded.com** REPLACE it with YOUR PayPal account name.

Step 2. Turn the Donate Box ON.

Turn the "Donate" Box ON or OFF, from the main Administration Menu shown on p. 12, select **Design Controls - InfoBox Admin**, then click the **Donate row**. Click the GREEN BUTTON to turn it ON or the RED BUTTON to turn it off. Click the UP or DOWN ARROW or LEFT or RIGHT arrow to move the box where you want.

 TIP: Alternatively, you may also click the EDIT Button at the BOTTOM of the InfoBox Admin screen, then update the info in the form boxes that appear at the bottom of the page.

Google AdSense SSL Safe Code

Allows you to display ads by Google and make money if your customers click it. This latest version eliminates the warning message about non-secure images when Google ads served in the secure checkout area.

 TIP: You must first set up an AdSense account with Google for this box to work. It only takes a minute!

Step 1. Get your Google AdSense account.

Go to http://www.google.com/adsense. Click the "**Click Here to Apply" Button** and create a username and password. Click "Individual Account" if you will have checks made out to you or "Business Account" for your company. Enter your address details on the "Account Information" page including website address, language, click the box, "Select AdSense for content if you want to run ads targeted to the content of your site" and click the SUBMIT Button. Wait 1-2 days for approval and an email telling you what to do next.

Step 2. Add your Google account numbers to your Google ads box.

Your account numbers are in the email you received. From the main Administration Menu shown on p. 12, select **Tools - Banner Manager**, then click **GOOGLE AD with the Group GOOGLEBOX** and click the **EDIT BUTTON.**

Banner Manager

Banners	Groups	Displays / Clicks	Status	Action
CRE	box-ad	42 / 0	○ ◉	⌁ ⓘ
CRE Loaded	box-ad	56 / 1	◉ ○	⌁ ⓘ
Google Ad	googlebox	113 / 0	◉ ○	⌁ ▶

TIP: Google AdSense is a TEXT AD! So you will only edit the box that says "HTML TEXT:"

In the HTML Text" Box, find this line in bold underline below, and replace it with your own ad client account number, being careful to NOT touch the " either before or after the account number: google_ad_client = "**pub-9120706631632888**";

If you have selected a channel, find this line in bold red below, and replace it with your own ad channel number, being careful to NOT touch the " either before or after the account number: google_ad_channel ="**1563076908**";

3. To activate your Google AdSense program InfoBox, from the main Administration Menu shown on p. 12, select **Design Controls - InfoBox Admin**, then click the Google Ad row. Click the GREEN BUTTON to turn it ON or the RED BUTTON to turn it off. Click the UP or DOWN ARROW or LEFT or RIGHT arrow to move the box where you want.

Who's Online InfoBox

This is different from the "Who's Online" in the Admin.

An InfoBox entitled "**Who's Online**" telling number of other customers in your store now. Turn on/off in Design Controls - InfoBox Admin

To use the Who's Online program, from the main Admin Menu shown on p. 12, select **DESIGN CONTROLS - InfoBox Admin.**

This brings you to the **InfoBox Admin menu**.

Find the row that says "Who's Online."

Click the GREEN BUTTON to turn the Who's Online InfoBox on.

Click the RED BUTTON to turn the Who's Online InfoBox off.

Who's Online

There currently are 5 guests and 1 member online.

Chapter

4

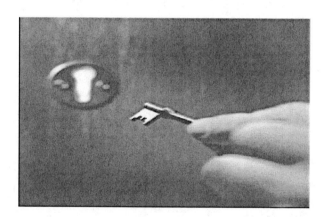

How to *Manage* Your Store
Using CRE Loaded 6.1 OSC

In this Chapter:

This chapter contains instructions on maintaining your store using the Administrative Module in CRE Loaded 6.1 version of osCommerce.

Level of difficulty: A breeze, like swinging in a hammock on a warm summer day.

We are again working through the main Administrative menu, this time in the **left-hand Store Management column as show on p. 12:**

a. My Account

The most important account is of course, yours. Change your own username or password here. CRE Loaded OSC knows that it's you, and automatically brings you to your account.

To change your name or password, from the main **Administrative Menu**, select **My Account – My Account/Password**. This brings you to the **Admin Account Menu**. Click the **EDIT button** to edit.

Before making any changes to your account, you must **enter your OLD password** and select the **CONFIRM button**:

Admin Account

This brings you to the **Admin Account** screen where you may edit any or all of your account information. Click the **SAVE button** when you are finished:

My Account	
Firstname:	My
Lastname:	Name
Email Address:	myname@myhost.com
Password:	
Confirm Password:	

Modified: 2004-10-02 23:31:20   back   save

b. Catalog Menu:

Categories/Products

There are several very important differences in these two menus. In CATEGORIES, you can edit using the "WYSIWYG" HTML Editor that makes it as easy to write category descriptions as writing an email.

Both the CATEGORIES and PRODUCTS menus have sections to automatically insert **Meta Tag Information.** The PRODUCTS section also uses the **Ultra-Pics contribution** which uploads Products images and additional Pop-Up images.

Meta Tags Information:

The CATEGORIES and PRODUCTS menus are similar. Products is shown below; from the main Admin menu shown on p. 12, select CATALOG – PRODUCTS. Click a product name to see this section in the middle of a product page:

a. Products Page Title :

> osCommerce Technical Manual:
> A Guide for Website Developers

a. Will display in the **top bar of the customer's browser**

b. Page Header Description :

> osCommerce Technical Manual shows the web developer everything you need to install, configure, customize, and add on

b. The text to **display on search engine results pages**

c. Product Keywords :

> oscommerce, oscommerce technical manua oscommerce technical guide, oscommerce book, handbook, installation, kerry watson

c. **The words people type into a search engine** to find your site.

Products Image Upload:

This allows you to upload images of different sizes and views with pop-up windows to enlarge. From the main Admin menu shown on p. 12, select CATALOG – PRODUCTS. Click a product name to see this section in the middle of a **product page. To begin uploading pictures,** click the **Picture Frame icon:**

Products Image:
Main Image used in
catalog & description
pages.

Choose Image

Small Image:
Image on
products list pages.

Pop-up Image:
Large Image on
pop-up window page.

Image Upload

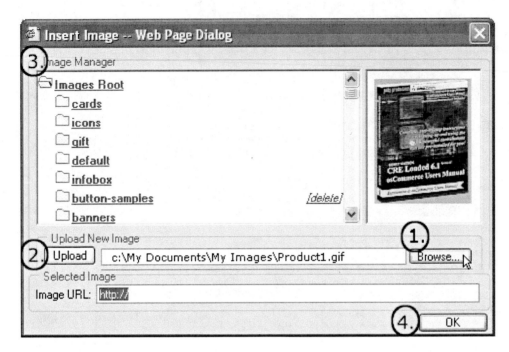

UPLOAD IMAGE TO YOUR WEBSITE:

STEP 1. Click the BROWSE Button and find the image on your computer.
STEP 2. Click the UPLOAD Button.

NOW TELL THE STORE "This is the image I want to display."

STEP 3. Scroll WAY DOWN until you find the image you just uploaded. CLICK IT and it will display in the "Selected Image box (the last box on the menu).
STEP 4. Click the OK Button.

Additional Images and Optional Pop-Up Enlargements

To add Additional Images and optional Pop-Up enlargements, in the menu below simply click the BROWSE Button. These additional images will not be uploaded until you save the product description. You should save your work every 15 minutes or CRE Loaded may "time out" to protect you for security reasons.

Additional Images - appear below product description if used.

SM = Small Images. If a "SM" image is used (Alone) NO Pop-up window link is created, the "SM" will be placed directly under the products description. If used in conjunction with an "XL" image on the right, a Pop-up Window Link is created and the "XL" image will be shown in a Pop-up window.

XL = Large Images. Used for the Pop-up image

SM Image 1:	_____	Browse...	XL Image 1:	_____	Browse...
SM Image 2:	_____	Browse...	XL Image 2:	_____	Browse...
SM Image 3:	_____	Browse...	XL Image 3:	_____	Browse...

EasyPopulate 2.75 Basic/Advanced

Easy Populate allows you to batch-upload, add or edit as many products as you wish, even thousands at a time, using a spreadsheet such as Microsoft Excel™ instead of the Administrative Module's slow, one-product-at-a-time method.

If your store has a large number of products and/or requires frequent updates of product information such as price changes or availability, then this is the ticket for you.

Product Name	Model	Price
$25 Gift Certificate	GIFT_25	$25.00
A Bug's Life	DVD-ABUG	$32.39
Beloved	DVD-BELOVED	$54.99
Blade Runner - Director's Cut	DVD-BLDRNDC	$35.99
Courage Under Fire	DVD-CUFI	$38.99
Die Hard With A Vengeance	DVD-DHWV	$25.00
Disciples: Sacred Lands	PC-DISC	$90.00
Fire Down Below		$29.99
Frantic		$32.00
Hewlett Packard		$499.99
Lethal Weapon		$34.99
Matrox G200 MM		$299.99
Matrox G400 32		$499.99
Microsoft IntelliM		$64.95
Microsoft IntelliM		$49.99
Microsoft Interne		$69.99
Red Corner		$31.00
Speed		$39.99
Speed 2: Cruise		$42.00
SWAT 3: Close		$79.99
The Matrix		$39.99
The Replacemen		$42.00

There are **two EasyPopulate methods**: BASIC and ADVANCED. You can download your products database by:

EasyPopulate 2.75 BASIC	EasyPopulate 2.75 ADVANCED
COMPLETE Products Database	COMPLETE Products Database
MODEL/PRICE/QTY only	MODEL/PRICE/QTY only
MODEL/CATEGORY only	MODEL/CATEGORY only
In FROOGLE format	In FROOGLE format
ATTRIBUTES ONLY	ATTRIBUTES ONLY
	Products in a certain Category
	Products by a certain Manufacturer
	Products sorted in a certain order

EasyPopulate Action Summary:	Administrative Module or Other Program:
1. BACKUP YOUR WEBSITE AND YOUR DATABASE. You will be making changes to the structure.	Use your FTP program for your web pages, phpMyAdmin or your web host's control panel for your database.
2. Use either basic or advanced version of EasyPopulate to (1) download your product database (or the portion you select)	CATALOG – EasyPopulate
3. make changes or additions to product information in any spreadsheet such as Excel,	Excel or other spreadsheet, save in TAB DELIMITED FORMAT
4. upload it again with EasyPopulate to replace the existing information.	Catalog – EasyPopulate.

TIP: See separate FROOGLE section that follows for details on exporting and using FROOGLE.

New in CRE 6.1: Product model numbers are no longer required; this version automatically uses products ID instead. Model numbers may now be up to 25 characters; previous versions required 12 characters or less.

TIP: Each row *must* end with EOREOR or only one product will upload. Each EasyPopulate file must also have a header row. If you upload a file without a header, it will assume your first row is the header and not upload the first product. *If you follow the directions in this book and first download your product database, even if it's empty, you do not have to worry about these things because the correct structure will already be in place.*

If you have ignored all my advice prior to this, do not ignore this one: BACK UP YOUR ENTIRE STORE AND DATABASE BEFORE PROCEEDING. You are going to be severely altering your database.

1. Backup your website and database.

Use your FTP program to GET a copy of your website.
Use phpMyAdmin or your web host's administrative panel to back up your entire database. Ask your web host for additional instructions.

2. Use Either Basic or Advanced EasyPopulate to Download (EXPORT) the file you will edit.

From the main Administrative Menu's **CATALOG** category, select **EASYPOPULATE** (basic or advanced). This brings you to the EasyPopulate menu. From here you will export the file to edit to your personal computer.

Importing the file gives you the correct file structure that you will need to later upload your products, even if your database is empty. DON'T SKIP THIS STEP!

TIP: "Tab-Delimited" means that there is a tab between each field, so when you import it into Excel all the columns will line up perfectly.

The first time you use this module, test it by downloading, adding ONE PRODUCT, and uploading. DON'T spend hours, days or weeks working on a file only to find you've done it wrong.

Under Item 1 below, Create an export file, click "DOWNLOAD," optionally select a field set to download, then click the START FILE CREATION button:

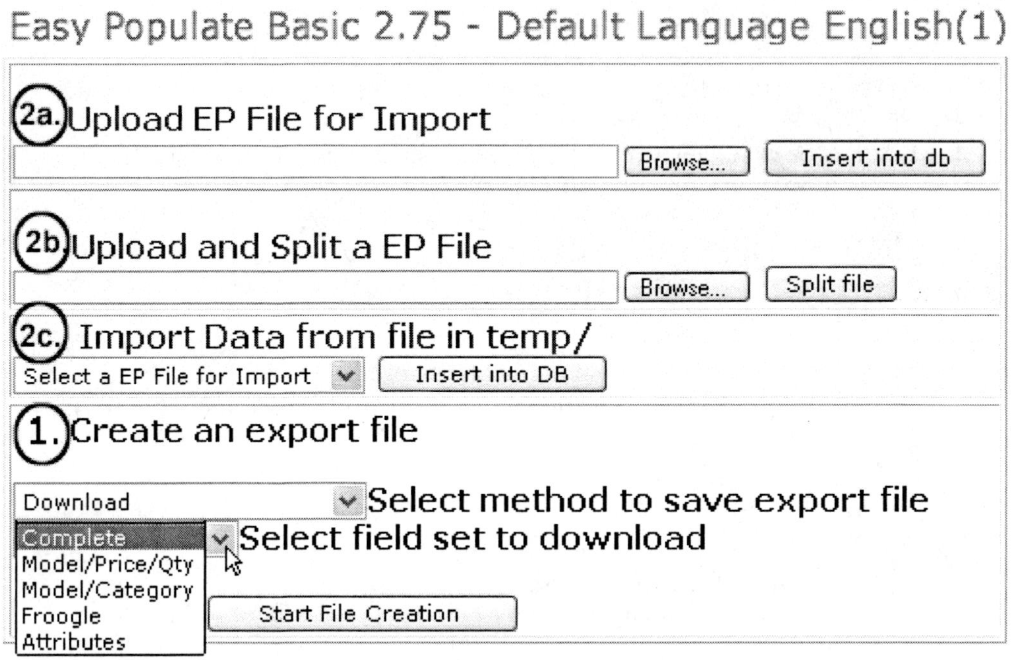

Easy Populate Basic 2.75 - Default Language English(1)

(2a.) Upload EP File for Import

[   ] [Browse...] [Insert into db]

(2b.) Upload and Split a EP File

[   ] [Browse...] [Split file]

(2c.) Import Data from file in temp/

[Select a EP File for Import ⌄] [Insert into DB]

(1.) Create an export file

[Download   ⌄] Select method to save export file

[Complete   ⌄] Select field set to download
| Model/Price/Qty |
| Model/Category |
| Froogle   [Start File Creation]
| Attributes

Save the file to your local computer:

You will receive the prompt to open or save it to your computer. Select **SAVE** and remember or write down the directory to which you saved it:

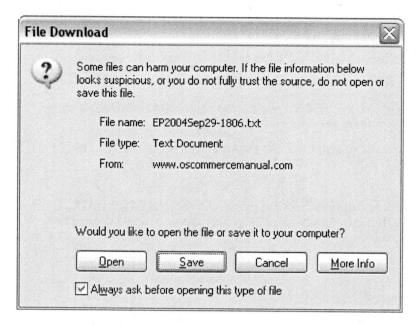

Next, **open Excel** or any spreadsheet of your choice. From here you may **add, edit, or delete products.**

After you finish editing, select **File-Save As** and *save the file as "TEXT (tab delimited).*

WARNING: YOUR FILE MUST BE SAVED AS A TAB-DELIMITED FILE. IF NOT AND YOU UPLOAD IT ANYWAY, YOU WILL TRASH YOUR ENTIRE ONLINE DATABASE.

DO NOT use an upload file created from a previous version of EasyPopulate. It will not have Product ID's and will try to read the model number as a product ID.

(Extra Step for Mac Users using EasyPopulate)

Apple uses a different end-of-line character than Unix or Windows. To change the end-of-line characters so they will be read correctly, after editing, simply open the file(s) in BBedit or a similar program and change the line endings to "UNIX."

3. Make Changes or Additions to Product Information in Any Spreadsheet such as Excel, Open Office

Use Excel, a spreadsheet such as Open Office, or another spreadsheet to edit your product information, and save in TAB DELIMITED FORMAT.

4. Upload the Edited Products File to Your Database:

Finally, you will upload your EasyPopulate file. From the main Administrative menu, select CATALOG – EASYPOPULATE (basic or advanced).

Find **item 2A** in the menu above entitled **UPLOAD EP FILE**, click its **BROWSE button**, find the file you just edited, and click the **INSERT INTO DB button.**

TIP: Uploading Images: EasyPopulate DOES NOT UPLOAD IMAGES FOR YOU. Use your FTP program to upload the image files separately.

(Alternate Upload Methods)

If your products file is very large, and you have difficulty with the upload hanging or not completing, you will need to use either method 2b or 2c in the picture above.

Method 2b, Upload and Split, splits a file into sections for you so that your database does not "time out" for security reasons.

Method 2c, Import Data from File in TEMP allows you to save the file to your store's /temp/ directory so it is much quicker to import to your store, again avoiding the "time out" issue.

Uploading - For All Methods:

You will see a display listing the items you are importing.

TIP: your last record often is blank. If you see an error message stating that EasyPopulate cannot import the last record, you can safely ignore it, it's about the blank record.

TIP: Make sure you have read-write-execute permission on the /temp/ directory. If not, temporarily CHMOD it to 777.

TIP: Blank Last Record- your last record often is blank. If you see an error message stating that EasyPopulate cannot import the last record, you can safely ignore it, it's about the blank record.

EasyPopulate Froogle Support:

Froogle is a search engine that finds and prices products that people want to buy. Using EasyPopulate, you can upload your store files to Froogle for FREE and get an increase in business.

Froogle   Results 1 - 50

OsCommerce
Technical
Manual: A Guide
$33.96 -

To use Froogle, there are five steps involved:
1) You simply sign up for a free Froogle account;
2) Get a Froogle FTP username and tell Froogle details about your file;
3) Use EasyPopulate to get a copy of your database in Froogle format;
4) Upload your products to the Froogle website, and
5) Check your file to be sure it has no errors.

Step 1. Sign up for a free Froogle account.

Go to http://www.google.com/froogle/merchants/
You will need to type in your current email address, select a password, and type the characters you see in an image to verify that you are a real person and not a machine. Verify that you have read the Terms of Service and Privacy Policy, and click the "Create My Account" Button.

Step 2. Get an FTP username and tell Froogle details about your file

a) From your Froogle Merchant Center Home page, click FTP and create an FTP Username and Password. Write down the name of the Froogle FTP Server and choose the FTP method that is easiest for you - there are several alternatives.

b) Click the link, "Register a New Product Feed" (NOT the Business Listings Feed!!!) and invent a name for your file. This is so Froogle will know which file goes to which store.

See this example: **Register a New Product Feed**

Store ID: Learn more

    kerrystore

Store Name: Learn more

    osCommerce Manuals

Store URL: Learn more

    http://www.oscommercemanuals.com

Adult Content:

    ☐

Filename (case sensitive): FroogleEP2005May29-1705.txt

    (eg "merry.txt", "merry_books.txt", or "merry.zip")

Currency

    US Dollar ▾

Language

    English ▾

    [Register new feed]   [Cancel]

Step 3. Use EasyPopulate to get a copy of your store's database in Froogle format.

Log onto your store, and from the main Admin menu, select CATALOG - EasyPopulate Basic. In the EasyPopulate "Create an export file" section, click the drop-down boxes so they say "Download" and "Froogle. Click the START FILE CREATION Button. Save the file to your Desktop with the same name you specified in Step 1.

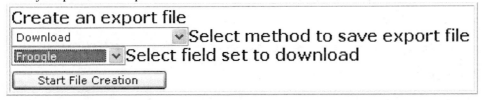

Create an export file

Download ▾ Select method to save export file

Froogle ▾ Select field set to download

[Start File Creation]

Step 4. Upload your products to the Froogle website

If you have not used FTP before, follow Froogle's excellent instructions to upload your file. Here is an example of an FTP program set up to upload the Froogle product feed:

Step 5. Check your file to be sure it has no errors.

Froogle advises waiting at least 3 hours before you check to see if your file was received. NOTE: If "OUTCOME" column says "ERRORS" click the "help" link.

Additional FROOGLE Help:	Location:
Glossary of Upload Error Messages:	http://www.google.com/support/froogle/bin/topic.py?topic=309
Google's well-written help:	https://www.google.com/froogle/merchants/getting_started.html
Froogle Support:	If you must email Froogle Support for help, be sure to contact them regularly, don't wait days for an answer: http://www.google.com/support/froogle
Froogle Merchants' Email group	http://groups-beta.google.com/ and join Froogle-Merchants@googlegroups.com

Specials

This module allows you to set special pricing temporarily, for certain products, categories, or your whole store.

To begin adding Specials to your store, from the main Administrative Menu's Catalog category, click **SPECIALS.** This takes you to the **SPECIALS Administration screen.** All your products that are currently on special will be listed in the left column:

Specials

Products	Products Price	Status	Action
A Bug's Life	$35.99 $32.39	○ ●	▶
Die Hard With A Vengeance	$39.99 $25.00	○ ●	ⓘ
Frantic	$35.00 $32.00	○ ●	ⓘ
Red Corner	$32.00 $31.00	○ ●	ⓘ

Displaying **1** to **4** (of **4** products on special)   Page 1 of 1

[new product]

To add new specials, click the NEW PRODUCT Button. Select the product to go on special from the PRODUCT drop-down box, enter a price and (optional) expiration date, and click the INSERT Button:

Specials

Product: You've Got Mail ($34.99) ▾

Special
Price:

Expiry
Date: ▢ ▢ ▢ ▷

[insert]   [cancel]

Shop by Price

Shop by Price
Under $30.00
$30.00 and above

Adds a "Shop by Price" InfoBox that allows customers to view items sorted by price.

Shop by Price is done in two steps:
1) set the total number of ranges you will want to display in the Options menu - in the above example there are a total of two (one, plus the "over-range" for $xx AND ABOVE. "
2) Specify the values for each range in the Range menu.

To use the Shop by Price program, from the main Admin Menu shown on p. 12, select **CATALOG - Shop By Price.**

Shop By Price

This brings you to the **Shop By Price** menu. Click the **EDIT button** to edit the OPTIONS settings, as follows:

Options:

Set the number of ranges to be supported. Optionally include an "and above" range.

Selection Ranges:

`0`

Automatic over range generation:

◉ True

○ False

[update] [cancel]

Step 1.

If you want it to add an extra range called "*$xx and above*" using the Automatic over-range generation feature, set the total number of ranges you want, minus one. In the example above, we have 1 range and 1 over-range, so we enter "1" in the Selection Ranges form box.

OTHERWISE, enter the exact number of ranges.

We want the "$xx and above" so set this to true.

Click the **UPDATE Button.**

Ranges:

The range limits must be in acending order.

Under `30.00`

[update] [cancel]

Step 2.

Open the SHOP BY PRICE RANGES Menu. Specify the value you want the first range to be. In the above example, it is "Under $30.00." Repeat if you want to add additional ranges.

Click the UPDATE Button.

The program generates the "over-range" automatically and shows you the amounts.

Cross Sell (X-Sell) Products

Customer's view of Cross Sell.

This powerful marketing module allows you to increase the total dollar sales of each customer by suggesting other related products.

 It is easier to sell more to each customer, than it is to get new customers.

To begin adding Cross-sale suggestions to your products, from the main Administrative Menu's Catalog category, click **CROSS SELL PRODUCTS**. This takes you to the **Cross-Sell (X-Sell) Administration screen**. All your products with their product ID's will be listed in the left column:

Cross-Sell (X-Sell) Admin

ID	Product Name	Cross-Associated Products	Cross Sell Actions		
33	osCommerce Technical Manual - Paperback	1. 10 Sneaky Tips & Tricks for osCommerce 2. osCommerce Users Manual V 2.0 - Paperback	Add	Remove	Sort

To add or remove a cross-sale suggestion, simply click **ADD or REMOVE**.

To specify the **order** in which a cross-sale suggestion will display, click **SORT** and specify the order.

SaleMaker

Use this module to set sale prices on ALL products in store, all products in a category, all products in a price range, and so forth. You may set price at a percentage off, a flat rate off, and for a specific time period to automatically start and end. You can have a holiday sale! Back to school sale! Birthday sale! And they will automatically appear and disappear on the days you specify.

To set a sale on merchandise in your store, from the **main Administrative Menu**, select **CATALOG – SALEMAKER.** This brings you to the **SALEMAKER page:**

SaleMaker

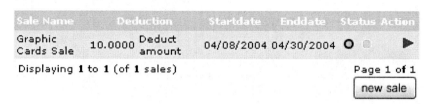

Sale Name	Deduction		Startdate	Enddate	Status	Action
Graphic Cards Sale	10.0000	Deduct amount	04/08/2004	04/30/2004	⊙ ○	▶

Displaying **1** to **1** (of **1** sales)   Page 1 of 1

[new sale]

From here you may add or edit a sale, as follows:

Sale Maker

Click here for Salemaker Usage Tips.   [insert]   [cancel]

SaleName: [   ]

Deduction: [   ] Type: [Deduct amount ▼]

Products Pricerange: [   ] To [   ]

If a product is a Special: [Ignore Specials Price ▼]

Start Date: [▼]

End Date: [▼]

Notice the built-in Help.

Give your sale a name.

Set the amount and type –
NOTE: MUST use a decimal point, i.e. 7.0 percent, 5.00 Deduct Amount.

Set a price range if desired, MUST use a decimal point, i.e. from 0.00 TO 10.00. Specify whether to markdown products already on sale, or ignore.

Set start date; if none, will start now.

Check this box if you want the sale to be applied to
► **all products**:

☐ Entire Catalog

Set end date; if none, will not expire.

Check to apply to entire catalog or specific categories. NOTE: Includes sub-categories.

► **Or** check the categories to which this sale applies:

☐ User Manuals

☐ Technical Manuals

☐ Cool Free Stuff

Featured Products

Featured Products allows you to select certain products to be displayed on the home page.

To select products to be featured on the home page, from the **main Administrative page,** select **Catalog – Featured Products.** This brings you to the **Featured Products screen**. To add products, click the **NEW PRODUCT button:**

Products	Status	Action

Displaying **0** to **0** (of **0** Featured Products) Page 0 of 0

[new product]

Step 1. Define the Product to be Featured.

Click the drop-down box to select the product, enter the date you want it to stop being featured (optional), and click the **INSERT button:**

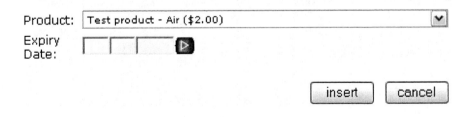

Featured Products

Product: | Test product - Air ($2.00) | ▼ |

Expiry Date: ☐ ☐ ☐ ▶

[insert] [cancel]

Step 2. Turn on the Featured Products Infobox.

In order for the Featured Products box to display on your home page, you must turn it on in the Template. From the main Administrative menu, select Design Controls – Infobox Admin. This brings you to the **Infobox Admin page**:

Simply click the **GREEN BUTTON** to turn on Featured Products.

Products Expected

This is simply an informational screen that makes it easy for stores that have entered products into the database with a "Future" stock date to keep track of those dates. This store has no scheduled arrivals:

Products Expected

Products	Date Expected	Action

Displaying **0** to **0** (of **0** products expected)   Page 0 of 0

c. Customers/Orders
Create New Account/New Order

This module allows you to manually add a new customer or new order if they place an order by means other than your website. Use it and you'll get a good reputation for good customer service, especially if a customer has accidentally aborted their transaction – such as closing their browser or timing out while they are making a purchase.

To add a new order, you must first add them as a customer.

1. Add (Create) a new customer:

From the main Administrative Menu's **CUSTOMERS/ORDERS** category, select **Create New Account.** This brings you to the **Add a New Customer** screen. Enter all the new customer information, just as if the customer were doing it.

2. Add (Create) a new order:

From the main Administrative Menu, select **Create New Order.**

STEP 1 - Choose a customer & check their details

Select a Customer:

[▼] [Select This Customer]

or Customer ID:

[ ] [Select This Customer ID]

Check Customer Details

If this is the right customer, press the Confirm button below.

ID:	[ ]	required
First Name:	[ ]	required
Last Name:	[ ]	required
E-Mail Address:	[ ]	required

The Customer Details will fill the screen below. Double-check to verify that this is the correct customer, and then click the **CONFIRM button** at the bottom.

This brings you to a very, very long screen called the Edit Order screen.

Edit Order Screen

Here you may either change the order, or click the **Add a New Product button** to add a product to the order. Note how the usual "Comments" box is at the bottom of this long screen; you may change the order status or write in comments as you normally do.

d. Reports Management Menu

Monthly Sales/Tax Reports

This is a robust report that lists a financial summary of all orders in the store database. NEW! **in 6.1: save the report to a spreadsheet with the click of a button; Print report; resort bottom to top (invert); and Help.**

Monthly Sales/Tax Summary Status: [All orders ▼]

Print   Invert   Help

Month	Year	Gross Income	Product sales	Exempt sales	Taxable sales	Tax paid	Shpg & Hndlg	Gift Vouchers
Jun	2004	0.00	0.00	0.00	0.00	0.00	0.00	135.00
May	2004	1,405.43	1,297.05	1,297.05	0.00	57.68	50.70	0.00
YTD	2004	3,882.79	3,365.15	3,365.15	0.00	159.39	223.25	135.00

Save CSV

For each **full** month, the report includes:

- **Gross Income** - the total of all sales, taxes and other charges
- **Product sales** - the total sales of products purchased
- **Exempt sales** - product sales which were shipped outside the store's zone
- **Taxable sales** - product sales which were shipped within the store's zone
- **Taxes paid** - the amount charged to customers for taxes
- **Shipping & handling** - the total shipping and handling charged
- **Low order fees** and/or **Gift Vouchers** - if enabled, totals are shown in their own columns.

Print Monthly Sales/Tax Report

To print the monthly sales/tax report, click the circled **PRINTER-FRIENDLY Print button.**

Get HELP/More Information on Monthly Sales/Tax Report

For an exact financial explanation of each column and how it is calculated, click the circled **HELP button.** Your accountant will also need this information; to **SAVE** the HELP page, **RIGHT-CLICK** on the page and select **FILE-SAVE AS.**

e. Tools Menu

Backup Database

This improved database backup tool backs up even the largest databases with ease. Previous versions had difficulty backing up larger stores that took longer than 30 seconds to download or upload, because that is the default length of time for PHP to timeout (or to close for security reasons). This new tool overcomes that problem.

To backup your database, from the main Administrative menu, select **Tools – Database Backup**. This brings you to the **Database Backup Manager:**

Database Backup

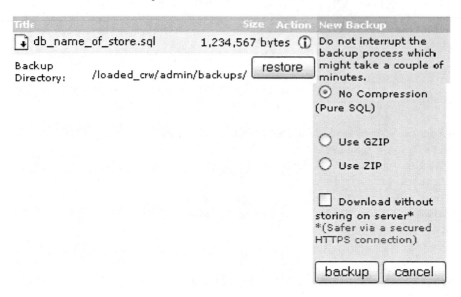

Click the **BACKUP button**, then the **BACKUP button** on the right to save to your local computer.

Email Customers

Send Email and Send Newsletters are both available in standard osCommerce, but as plain text only. In CRE Loaded osCommerce 6.1 you can send HTML email – email with special fonts, colors, images, just like a web page.

Both **Send Email** and **Send Newsletters** work in the identical way, so only one is shown here.

To send email or newsletters to your customers, from the main **Administrative Menu,** select **Tools – Send Email (or Send Newsletters).** This brings you to the **Email Customers** (or Newsletters) screen:

Send Email To Customers

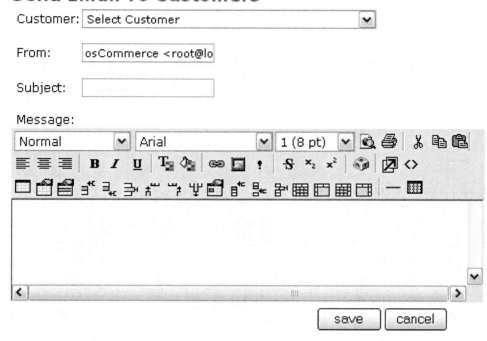

You may email **one or all customers**, or **one or all newsletter subscribers**.

Enter the text as usual, specifying fonts, colors, etc. and inserting the pictures of your choice. After you click the **SAVE button**, you will have the choice to **SEND or CANCEL**.

TIP: SEND the email to yourself as a test; sometimes the messages will not look as you expected!

CAUTION: **TIP: Be very careful emailing to non-subscribers. The CAN-SPAM Act of 2003 requires, among other things, that you unsubscribe recipients who request it. Fines can reach $10,000 for each infraction. YOU ARE RESPONSIBLE for compliance with this law. Find out more by searching on the web for CAN-SPAM.**

f. Affiliates Management Menu

Affiliate program is a powerful additional channel to sell your products on the web. People who want to sell your product sign up to be affiliates, you set a commission, either a flat fee or a percentage. They post your ad banners on their website. The banners have their "affiliate code" linked to them and CRE-Loaded tracks who comes to the site from the affiliate and who ultimately purchases your products. The affiliate sales are tallied by the program and you make payments to affiliates on a regular basis.

Affiliate Program

Affiliate Information
Affiliate Log In

Affiliates Action Summary:	Administrative Module:
1. Upload your ad banners	AFFILIATES - BANNERS
2. Set your affiliate commissions and program details in the Configuration Menu.	CONFIGURATION – AFFILIATE PROGRAM
3. **OPTIONAL:** Set custom affiliate informational messages	Done manually in /includes/ languages/YOUR LANGUAGE/ affiliate_*.php
4. **OPTIONAL:** Customize the Affiliate *Signup* email sent to new affiliates	/includes/languages/YOUR LANGUAGE/affiliate_signup_ok.php
5. **OPTIONAL:** Customize the Affiliate *Welcome* email sent to new affiliates	/includes/languages/YOUR LANGUAGE/affiliate_signup_ok.php
6. Enable or disable Affiliates InfoBox	DESIGN CONTROLS – InfoBox Admin - click GREEN button next to Affiliates.

Step 1. Upload your ad banners for affiliates

Create a variety of ad banners for your website or your product(s) using a graphics program such as PhotoShop. Standard sizes are 468x60 for banners, and 125x125 for "button" ads in left or right columns. However, you may make them any size you wish.

Once you have your banners ready, from the main **Administrative Menu** click **BANNERS** to get to the Affiliate Banner Manager.

Affiliate Banner Manager

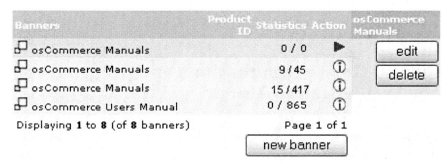

Banners	Product ID	Statistics	Action	osCommerce Manuals
osCommerce Manuals	0 / 0	▶		edit
osCommerce Manuals	9 / 45	ⓘ		delete
osCommerce Manuals	15 / 417	ⓘ		
osCommerce Users Manual	0 / 865	ⓘ		

Displaying **1** to **8** (of **8** banners)   Page 1 of 1

new banner

From the Affiliate Banner Manager, click the **NEW BANNER button.** This takes you to the **NEW BANNER page.**

NOTE: These banners are to be "picked up" by affilates; they will not display on your website.

Affiliate Banner Manager

Banner Title: | osCommerce Manuals | * Required

Product ID | 31 |

If you want to link the Banner to a specific product enter its Products ID here. If you want to link to the default page enter "0"

Image: | C:\Documents and Set | Browse... | , or enter local file from your server below
/phesis/images/ | |

Image Target (Save To):   /phesis/images/ | |

insert   cancel

1. Banner Title: Create a title for your ad. NOTE: This will show up on your affiliates' sites as the ALT TEXT.

2. Product ID: If you want to link directly to a product, enter it here. Find your product numbers quickly by opening your catalog, going to the product, and looking in the address bar for ?productid=

3. Image: Click the **BROWSE button** to select the ad from your computer.

4. Click the **INSERT button.**

Repeat this process to upload each of your ads.

Step 2. Set your affiliate commissions and program details in the Configuration Menu.

The affiliate program *configuration* is done using the **Configuration Menu**. From the main Administrative menu, select **Configuration – Affiliate Program**. This brings you to the Affiliate Program screen:

Affiliate Program

Title	Value
E-Mail Address	<affiliate@localhost.com>
Affiliate Pay Per Sale Payment % Rate	10.0000
Payment Threshold	50.00
Cookie Lifetime	7200
Billing Time	30
Order Min Status	3
Pay Affiliates with check	true
Pay Affiliates with PayPal	true
Pay Affiliates by Bank	true
Individual Affiliate Percentage	true
Use Affiliate-tier	false
Number of Tierlevels	0
Percentage Rate for the Tierlevels	8.00;5.00;1.00

Enter the email address you want to display in correspondence with affiliates.
Enter Per sale flat rate or percentage.
Minimum sales to generate a check to affiliate.
Maximum number of cookies from an affiliate.
Frequency of payments to affiliates.
Minimum order status, 3=delivered
Types of payments to make.
Allow tiers? (i.e. sub-affiliates)
Set rates for each tier.

**The Configuration Menu's
Affiliate Program Setup.**

OPTIONAL: Step 3. Set affiliate informational messages

OPTIONAL: Customize what you want to tell potential affiliates using your HTML editor. Be sure to include information on percentages you offer, how often you will pay affiliates, and so forth.

TIP: This step is optional. If you are not comfortable editing a line of php, draft the custom text you want and send it to your installer to do.

Always backup before editing a program file!!!

Open the file /includes/languages/YOUR LANGUAGE/affiliate_info.php **and**

Search for this line	define('TEXT_INFORMATION', **'Your affilates text goes here.'**);
and change it to	define('TEXT_INFORMATION', **'Whatever You Want to Say Here'**);

OPTIONAL: Step 4. Customize the Affiliate *Signup* email sent to new affiliates

An email is automatically sent to each person who signs up to be an affiliate. You may optionally customize this if you wish; here's how:

Open the file
/includes/languages/YOUR LANGUAGE/affiliate_signup_ok.php
and

Search for this line	define('TEXT_INFORMATION', **'Congratulations! Your new Affiliate account application has been submitted! You will shortly receive an email containing important information regarding your Affiliate Account, including you affiliate login details. If you have not received it within the hour, please <a href="'** . tep_href_link(FILENAME_AFFILIATE_CONTACT) . **'">contact us</a>. If you have <small>ANY</small> questions about the affiliate program, please <a href="'** . tep_href_link(FILENAME_AFFILIATE_CONTACT) . **'">contact us</a>.'**);
and change it to	define('TEXT_INFORMATION', **'Whatever you want to say here'**);

OPTIONAL: Step 5. Customize the Affiliate *Welcome* email sent to new affiliates

Open the file
/includes/languages/YOUR LANGUAGE/affiliate_signup_ok.php
and

Search for this line	define('MAIL_AFFILIATE_HEADER', **'Dear Affiliate,**
	
	thank you for joining the Affiliate Program.
	
	Your Account Information:
	**********************
	
	');
	define('MAIL_AFFILIATE_ID', 'Your Affiliate ID is: ');
	define('MAIL_AFFILIATE_USERNAME', 'Your Affiliate Username is: ');
	define('MAIL_AFFILIATE_PASSWORD', 'Your Password is: ');
	define('MAIL_AFFILIATE_LINK', 'Link to your account here:');
	define('MAIL_AFFILIATE_FOOTER', 'Have fun earning referal fees!
	
	Your Affiliate Team');

and change	The text shown above in **BOLD**.

Step 6. Turn on Affiliates Program Infobox:

Your new Affiliates Program will not display on your website until you tell it to. From the main **Administrative Menu**, select **Design Controls – Infobox Admin**. This brings you to the **Infobox Display, Create and Update Menu**.

From here, find **Affiliate Info** and click the Green button to Activate Box:

Infobox Display, Create and Update

Original ▾

Title	Font Color	Activate Box?	Set Column	Box Template	Box Heading Define	Position	Action
Categories	○ ●	⬅ ⇨	infobox	BOX_HEADING_CATEGORIES	⬇	▶
Affiliate Info	● ○	⬅ ⇨	infobox	BOX_HEADING_AFFILIATE	⬆ ⬇	Ⓒ

Your affiliate program is now complete and live.

Affiliate Reports

The affiliates program contains a number of reports so you can track how your affiliates are doing. All reports are accessed from the Main Administrative Menu under the AFFILATES category show on p. 12.

Affiliates Summary Menu

This is a summary report listing the number of affiliates you have, how many viewers have seen your banners on affiliate sites, how many sales have resulted from affiliate sites, and so forth.

Most revealing is the Conversion Rate, or the percentage of customers you get as a result of clicking to your site from an affiliate. Typical industry averages are less than 1%. Many affiliate programs enjoy double that amount or more. This tells you that you will get twice the return on your investment if you work on recruiting affiliates, compared to your return if you pay for typical advertising on other websites.

Affiliate Summary

Number of Affiliates:	26		
Total Banner Impressions: [?]	n/a	Total Affiliate Visits: [?]	1648
Total Affiliate Transactions: [?]	36	Conversion: [?]	2.18%
Total Affiliate Sales: [?]	$1,400.25	Average Affiliate Payout/Sale: [?]	$38.90
Commission Rate: [?]	20 %	**Total Affiliate Commission :** [?]	**$280.05**

Click on [?] to see a description of each category.

[build banner]　[clickthrough report]　[sales report]

Affiliates Payment Menu

This report allows you to see payments you have made to each affiliate.

Affiliates Sales Menu

This report allows you to see the sales you have received from each affiliate.

Affiliate Sales

Affiliate	Date	Order_ID	Value	Commission Rate	Sales	Status
Salvatore Iozzia	09/27/2004	608	$0.00	20.00%	$0.00	Pending
Salvatore Iozzia	09/27/2004	607	$0.00	20.00%	$0.00	Pending

Displaying **1** to **10** (of **116** sales)   << Page 1 ▾ of 12 >>

Affiliate Click-Through Report

This report allows you to see which affiliates are sending you the most traffic, where they came from, what browser and operating system they are using:

Affiliate Clickthroughs

Affiliate / IP Address	Date / Refering URL	Clicked Product	Browser
Salvatore Iozzia 82.150.72.37	09/27/2004	Startpage	Mozilla/4.0 (compatible; MSIE 6.0; Windows NT 5.1; .NET CLR 1.1.4322)
Salvatore Iozzia 83.157.198.99	09/27/2004 http://www.creloaded.com/modules.php? name=Content&pa=showpage&pid=8	Startpage	Mozilla/4.0 (compatible; MSIE 6.0; Windows 98; .NET CLR 1.1.4322)

Displaying **1** to **10** (of **1650** clickthroughs)   << Page 1 ▼ of 165 >>

Affiliates Contact Menu

You should keep in regular contact with your affiliates to keep their interest and keep them sending you traffic. This menu allows you to send email to one or all affiliates.

Send Email to Affiliates

Affiliate: [All Affiliates ▼]

From: [yourname@yourwebsite.com]

Subject: [   ]

Message: [   ]

[send mail]

g. FAQ Desk

Once your store starts growing, you may find that you need one FAQ for sales, another for customer service after the sale, another for technical support. This contribution is ideal for active FAQ management where you can easily add questions "on the fly." You can even have sub-FAQ's underneath your top level FAQ's. Your imagination is the limit!

Your customers will like this feature because they can easily search for a list of FAQ answers, and can leave reviews of each answer. Use the reviews feature to refine your replies and cut down even more on customer emails, confusion and lost sales.

FAQ's work very much like categories and products: the category is like the FAQ name, and the products are like the FAQ questions. Like products, you start by defining a FAQ name, then adding questions.

You must enable the FAQ to display using the Info System Info Manager, then set the configuration settings in Listing Settings and the home page settings in Front Page Settings.

FAQ Desk Action Summary:	Administrative Module:
1. Create FAQ	FAQ Desk – FAQDESK MGMT
2. Create FAQ question(s)	FAQ Desk – FAQDESK MGMT
3. Set FAQ Home Page configuration	FAQDESK MGMT – Front Page Settings
4. Set FAQ general listing configuration	FAQDESK MGMT – Listing Settings
4. Enable or disable FAQ InfoBox to display	DESIGN CONTROLS – Infobox Admin – click GREEN button next to FAQ.
5. Enable or disable a specific FAQ to display	FAQDesk MGMT – navigate to the FAQ and click the GREEN button.

From the main **Administrative Menu,** select **FAQ Desk – FAQDESK MGMT.** This brings you to the **FAQ Desk Management menu.**

FAQDesk Management

The example below has two FAQ's entitled Support FAQ and Sales FAQ.

To add questions to the Support FAQ, click the FILE FOLDER 🗀 and then select the **NEW FAQ** BUTTON.

TIP: If you forget to click the FILE FOLDER and put your
question in the wrong FAQ, simply highlight the question
and click MOVE.

FAQDesk... Category and
FAQ Management

This brings you to the **FAQ Question Management menu:**

FAQDesk... Category and
FAQ Management

To add a new FAQ beneath the current FAQ, click NEW CATEGORY.

To edit a question, highlight it in the Action column and click the **EDIT BUTTON.**

To delete a question, highlight it in the Action column and click the **DELETE BUTTON.**

To delete a question, highlight it in the Action column and click the **EDIT BUTTON.**

To delete a question, highlight it in the Action column and click the **EDIT BUTTON.**

**To KEEP A FAQ QUESTION AT THE TOP OF THE CURRENT FAQ, in the STICKY
column click the GREEN BUTTON.**

FAQ Desk Reviews Management

If you have enabled FAQ Reviews by customers, you will want to review and approve them before they go live. To approve reviews, from the main Administrative Menu select FAQ Desk – Reviews Management.

If you have pending reviews for you to edit, click the **EDIT button,** make changes if you wish, and select **UPDATE button.**

If you need to delete a review, for example due to vulgar language, select the review and click the **DELETE button.**

FAQ Reviews

FAQS	Rating	Date Added	Approved	Action

Displaying **0** to **0** (of **0** product reviews)   Page 0 of 0

FAQ Initial Setup

FAQ Listing Settings

This is the configuration page for the FAQ module. The default is shown below. It's not necessary to tweak these settings unless you wish to change them:

FAQ Listing Settings

Title	Value	Action	Search Results
Search Results	20	▶	edit
Page Links	5	ⓘ	
Display Question	1	ⓘ	How many FAQS
Display Short Answer	2	ⓘ	do you want to list?
Display Long Answer	3	ⓘ	
Display Date	4	ⓘ	Date Added: 02/16/2003
Location of Prev/Next Navigation Bar	3	ⓘ	

FAQ Front Page Settings

This menu sets the look of the FAQ InfoBox on your Home Page. The default is shown below. It's not necessary to tweak these settings unless you wish to change them:

FAQ Front Page Settings

Title	Value	Action	Display Main FAQS Items
Display Main FAQS Items	3	▶	
Latest FAQS Box Counts	5	ⓘ	**edit**
Display Latest FAQS Box	1	ⓘ	
Display FAQS Catagory Box	1	ⓘ	How many FAQS do you want to display on the top page?
Display View Counts	1	ⓘ	
Display Read More	1	ⓘ	
Display Short Answwer	1	ⓘ	Date Added: 02/16/2003
Display Question	1	ⓘ	
Display Date	1	ⓘ	
Display Image 1	1	ⓘ	
Display Image 2	1	ⓘ	
Display Image 3	1	ⓘ	

FAQ Reviews Settings

If you wish to enable or disable the display of reviews your customers write about each FAQ question, enable this module by clicking the EDIT BUTTON and entering 1 to enable and 0 to disable, then clicking the UPDATE button.

FAQ Display Reviews

Reviews Settings

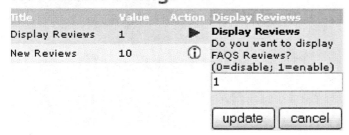

Title	Value	Action	Display Reviews
Display Reviews	1	▶	**Display Reviews** Do you want to display FAQS Reviews? (0=disable; 1=enable)
New Reviews	10	ⓘ	1

update   cancel

Number of FAQ Reviews to Display

To change the number of FAQ reviews that are automatically displayed about each FAQ question, enable this module by clicking the item in the ACTION column, entering the number of reviews you want to display, then clicking the UPDATE button.

Reviews Settings

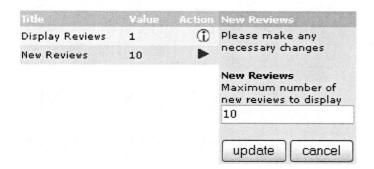

Title	Value	Action	New Reviews
Display Reviews	1	ⓘ	Please make any necessary changes
New Reviews	10	▶	

New Reviews
Maximum number of new reviews to display

`10`

[update] [cancel]

FAQ Sticky Settings

To change the settings for the items that remain at the top of your FAQ (STICKY items), from the main Administrative Menu, select FAQDesk – STICKY SETTINGS. Below are the default values; to change, simply click the **Action** column and then click the **EDIT button:**

FAQ Sticky Settings

Title	Value	Action	Display Question
Display Question	1	▶	[edit]
Display Short Answer	1	ⓘ	
Display Long Answer	1	ⓘ	Do you want to display the question?
Display View Counts	1	ⓘ	(0=disable; 1=enable)
Display Read More	1	ⓘ	
Display Date	1	ⓘ	
Display URL	1	ⓘ	Date Added: 03/02/2003
Display Image	1	ⓘ	
Display Image 2	1	ⓘ	
Display Image 3	1	ⓘ	

Other FAQ Settings

Currently the only item in this menu is to allow or disallow category (FAQ) descriptions. If you don't want to provide an explanation of what the FAQ contains – for example, if the title is SUPPORT FAQ you don't need to explain it in a paragraph too – disable it by clicking the **EDIT button** and change the value to **false:**

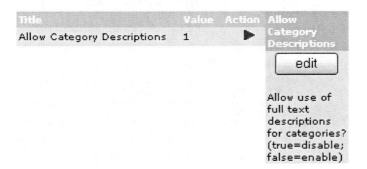

h. Gift Vouchers/Coupons

This complex set of contributions work together to allow your customers to redeem coupons or gift vouchers by entering coupon codes into a box presented during checkout. The Credit Class system adds some necessary functions to the Order Total class. The Gift Voucher system and the Discount Coupons system use these classes.

Setting up gift voucher/coupons is a **two step process**. First, you will **create** it either using the Administrative Module's Gift Vouchers/Coupons module, OR using the Catalog - Products module (your choice). You then **enable** it using the Administrative Module's MODULES – ORDER TOTAL - menu.

Optionally, you may also elect to send a New Customer Discount to all new customers in the Welcome Email, simply by enabling it in the Administrative Module's Configuration – My Store module.

Gift Certificate/Coupon Action Summary:	Administrative Module:
1. Create Gift Voucher/Coupon	Use EITHER Gift Vouchers/Coupons module, OR products module (your choice).

2. Enable Gift Voucher/Coupon	Modules – Order Total
3. Administer Gift Voucher/Coupons	Gift Vouchers/Coupons – Coupon Admin
4. OPTIONAL: Enable New Customer Discount in Welcome Gift Voucher	Configuration – My Store
5. OPTIONAL: Edit Welcome Email Gift Voucher text	ADVANCED USERS ONLY - See PHP editing instructions that follow.
6. NOT OPTIONAL: TEST to be sure this works fully with your payment module.*	Create a low-priced fake product and actually purchase it using a gift certificate/coupon.

CAUTION: *CAUTION: Some payment modules may lack support for portions of this feature. Each store owner must carefully test this system with his or her payment module of choice before placing it in use. If the test fails, try changing the Order Total - Sort Order until it works.**

1. Create Gift Voucher/Coupons

To create or administer gift vouchers/coupons, from the main **Admin Menu's Gift Vouchers/Coupons** module select **COUPON ADMIN.** This brings you to the **Discount Coupons menu:**

Discount Coupons

Coupon Name	Coupon Amount	Coupon Code	Action
New Customer	20.0000%	NEW	▶

Displaying 1 to 5 (of 5 coupons)   Page 1 of 1

> insert

To create a new coupon, click the **INSERT button.**

Optional Method: Create Gift Voucher using the Products Menu:

A gift voucher or gift certificate is a product that your customers can purchase, just like any other product. Therefore, you can create it exactly as you would create any other product – in the **Catalog Category-Product** menu.

For your convenience, a $25 gift certificate is correctly pre-installed for you in CRE-Loaded:

To use it, simply enable it by going to the **Administrative Menu's Catalog** category, selecting **PRODUCTS**, highlighting the certificate product and clicking the **GREEN BUTTON**.

TIP: Gift certificate images are pre-installed for denominations of $25, $50 and $100 in the directory /images/.

TIP: For the program to KNOW that a product is a gift certificate, it must have a product model number starting with GIFT in upper case letters. Examples of correct model names: GIFT_CERTIFICATE, GIFT_10, GIFTANYTHING.

2. Enable Gift Vouchers/Discount Coupons

To enable gift vouchers/discount coupons, from the main **Administrative menu,** select **Modules – ORDER TOTAL.** This brings you to the **ORDER TOTAL MODULES** menu.

To enable the gift vouchers or discount coupons, select the item under **ACTION** and then click the **INSTALL button:**

Order Total Modules

This brings you to the **Gift Vouchers** menu. Click the **EDIT button** to edit and then fill in as follows:

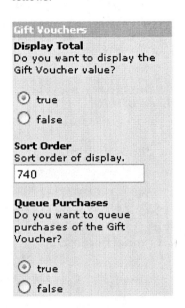

Must be set to TRUE.

Leave at suggested sort order.

If fraud (redeeming vouchers after receiving refund) is a concern, set to TRUE. See gift certificate administration to redeem. If FALSE, certificate will immediately be available for redemption without your approval.

Include Shipping
Include Shipping in
calculation

◉ true

○ false

Include Tax
Include Tax in calculation.

◉ true

○ false

Re-calculate Tax
Re-Calculate Tax

◉ None

○ Standard

○ Credit Note

Tax Class
Use the following tax class
when treating Gift Voucher as
Credit Note.

[--none-- ▼]

Credit including Tax
Add tax to purchased Gift
Voucher when crediting to
Account

○ true

◉ false

[update] [cancel]

Set to TRUE if you wish to permit customers to pay for shipping with their gift certificates.

Set to TRUE if you wish to permit customers to pay for tax with their gift certificates.

RE-CALCULATE TAX - Set to NONE unless required by your local tax laws. Check with your accountant or attorney to be sure you are collecting taxes properly on gift certificates. If advised to change, the two options give slightly different results:

STANDARD - Recalculates the tax on any taxable elements after deduction of the Gift Voucher amount.

CREDIT NOTE - recalculates the tax by considering the Gift Voucher amount as a Credit Note.

TAX CLASS – set if using Credit Note method.
CREDIT INCLUDING TAX – leave FALSE to avoid anomalies where purchase of certificate is taxed, giving a total gift certificate credit of the amount of the certificate PLUS TAX (ie if tax is 10%, the gift certificate face value would be $11.)

Enable Discount Coupons

Coupons are similar to gift vouchers, except they are not offered as products that customers can purchase on your website. Follow the instructions above for Gift Vouchers, simply substituting the following menu in **MODULES - ORDER TOTAL:**

Order Total Modules

Modules	Sort Order	Action	Discount
Discount Coupons	1	▶	Coupons
Gift Vouchers		ⓘ	— remove
Low Order Fee		ⓘ	edit
Shipping		ⓘ	

Discount Coupons

Display Total
Do you want to display the Discount Coupon value?

◉ true
○ false

Display Total - Must be set to TRUE.

Sort Order
Sort order of display.

| 1 |

Leave at default sort order.

Include Shipping
Include Shipping in calculation

○ true
◉ false

Include Shipping - Set to TRUE if you wish to permit customers to pay for shipping with their gift certificates.

Include Tax
Include Tax in calculation.

○ true
◉ false

Include Tax - Set to TRUE if you wish to permit customers to pay for tax with their gift certificate.

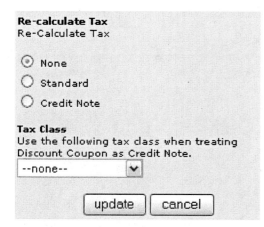

Re-Calculate Tax - Set to NONE unless required by your local tax laws. Check with your accountant or attorney to be sure you are collecting taxes properly on gift certificates. If advised to change, the two options give slightly different results:
Standard - Recalculates the tax on any taxable elements after deduction of the Gift Voucher amount.
Credit Note - recalculates the tax by considering the Gift Voucher amount as a Credit Note.
Tax Class – set if using Credit Note method. Click **UPDATE button** when finished.

3. Administer Coupons/Gift Vouchers

Once you have coupons/gift vouchers set up, administration involves emailing new vouchers to customers, redeeming queued vouchers (if you have enabled queueing in the Modules - Order Total menu), and checking your report of gift vouchers sent.

Email Gift Voucher

To send a gift voucher to a customer, from the main Administrative Menu, select GIFT VOUCHERS/COUPONS – EMAIL GIFT VOUCHER. This brings you to the Send Gift Voucher to Customers menu.

TIP: You cannot send a gift voucher to a NON-customer using this menu. First enter the customer information in the CUSTOMERS/ ORDERS – Create New Account menu.

Everything in this menu is self-explanatory except for the **AMOUNT** box. Simply enter the amount of the Gift Voucher.

TIP: You MUST enter the name of the Gift Voucher/Coupon in the text of your message and explain to the customer how to redeem their coupon.

SAMPLE GIFT EMAIL MESSAGE TEXT:

"To redeem your gift certificate, go to www.mystore.com and select the item(s) you wish to purchase with your certificate. When checking out, in the GIFT CERTIFICATE box, simply enter the gift certificate code GIFT-25."

Send Gift Voucher to Customers

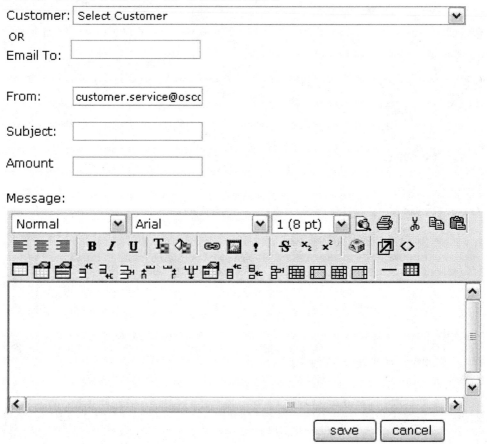

Gift Voucher Queue

To help prevent fraud by someone purchasing a gift certificate, canceling payment, and then redeeming the certificate, FIRST check the payment status of the purchase to be sure the purchaser did not request a refund, THEN release the gift voucher.

TIP: To use this menu you must have first enabled queueing in the Administrative menu's MODULES – ORDER TOTAL menu; see the previous section.

To permit your customers to use their gift voucher, highlight the customer order number and click the **REDEEM** button:

Gift Voucher Release Queue

Customers Order-No. Voucher Value Date Purchased Action	[] $0.00

Displaying **0** to **0** (of **0** gift vouchers)　　　　Page 0 of 0　　[Redeem]

Gift Vouchers Sent

To see a list of gift vouchers you or other customers have sent, from the main Administrative Menu's **GIFT VOUCHERS/COUPONS** section select **Gift Vouchers Sent.**

This brings you to the **GIFT VOUCHERS SENT** menu:

Gift Vouchers Sent

Senders Name	Voucher Value	Voucher Code	Date Sent Action	[6] $2.50
Admin	$2.50	b32ee	9/28/2004　▶	Senders ID: 0
				Amount Sent: $2.50
Displaying **1** to **1** (of **1** gift vouchers)			Page 1 of 1	Date Sent: 09/28/2004
				Voucher Code: b32ee
				Email Addr:
				couponlover@asite.com
				Not Redeemed

The menu is self-explanatory except for the following: redemption status (Redeemed/Not Redeemed) is listed at the bottom right. See above example.

4. (Optional) Enable New Customer Welcome Message Gift Voucher

When customers register with your store, they receive a standard automatic Welcome email from you. If you wish to include a welcome Gift Voucher, from the main Administrative Menu, select **Configuration – My Store.** This brings you to the **My Store configuration menu**. Select Welcome Gift Voucher Amount by clicking the Action column and click the EDIT button:

My Store

Title	Value	Action
Default theme	Original	ⓘ
Store Name	osCommerce	ⓘ
Store Owner	Harald Ponce de Leon	ⓘ
Store Logo	oscommerce.gif	ⓘ
E-Mail Address	root@localhost	ⓘ
E-Mail From	osCommerce <root@localhost>	
Featured Products on Main Page	United States	ⓘ
Display Prices with Tax	false	ⓘ
Welcome Gift Voucher Amount	0	▶
Welcome Discount Coupon Code		ⓘ
Category/Products Display Order	PRODUCT_LIST_MODEL	ⓘ

This brings you to the **Welcome Gift Voucher Configuration** menu. Enter the amount of gift voucher you want to send new customers and click UPDATE:

Welcome Gift Voucher Amount

Please make any necessary changes

Welcome Gift Voucher Amount
Welcome Gift Voucher Amount: If you do not wish to send a Gift Voucher in your create account email put 0 for no amount else if you do place the amount here i.e. 10.00 or 50.00 no currency signs

```
0
```

Next, **create a coupon code** that will be sent to your new customers in the welcome email. They will be instructed to enter this coupon code when checking out:

Welcome Discount Coupon Code

Please make any necessary
changes

Welcome Discount Coupon Code
Welcome Discount Coupon
Code: if you do not want to send
a coupon in your create account
email leave blank else place the
coupon code you wish to use

[   ]

[update]   [cancel]

Select the **UPDATE button** to complete the Welcome Email Gift Certificate configuration.

5. OPTIONAL: Customize the Welcome Discount Email

TECHNICAL STUFF WARNING: Unless you love the technical stuff, this is something that a programmer or technical person should do for you.

Open file **includes/languages/english/create_account.php** and edit any section below shown in **BOLD**.

Search for:
```
define('EMAIL_GV_INCENTIVE_HEADER', 'As part of our welcome to new
customers, we have sent you an e-Gift Voucher worth %s');
define('EMAIL_GV_REDEEM', 'The redeem code for is %s, you can enter the
redeem code when checking out, after making a purchase');
define('EMAIL_GV_LINK', 'or by following this link ');
define('EMAIL_COUPON_INCENTIVE_HEADER', 'Congratulations, to make your
first visit to our online shop a more rewarding experience' . "\n" .
  ' below are details of a Discount Coupon created just for you' .
"\n\n");
define('EMAIL_COUPON_REDEEM', 'To use the coupon enter the redeem code
which is %s during checkout, ' . "\n" .
                    'after making a purchase');
```

CAUTION: **CAUTION: Replace ONLY THE TEXT in the message, being careful to not erase any codes. DO NOT MANUALLY ALTER REDEEM CODE or DOLLAR AMOUNT HERE - use the Administrative Module instructions above.**

6. *NOT* OPTIONAL: TEST to be sure this works fully with your payment module.

Create a low-priced fake product and go through entire purchase process using the gift voucher or coupon.

CAUTION: **CAUTION: Some payment modules may lack support for portions of this feature. Each store owner must carefully test this system with his or her payment module of choice before placing it in use. If the test fails, try changing the Order Total - Sort Order until it works.**

i. News Desk Management Menu

Keep customers returning to your store by regularly publishing news about your industry or store. This contribution is a powerful news content management system that allows you to easily add articles "on the fly." *You could even use it to manage an entire website.*

Your customers will like this feature because they can easily search for a list of news articles, and can leave reviews of each article. Use the reviews feature to refine your replies and cut down even more on customer emails, confusion and lost sales.

News Desk works very much like the FAQ Desk and like categories and products: the category is the news category name, and the articles are the news articles. Like products, you start by defining a news category name, then adding questions.

You must enable the News InfoBox to display using the Info System Info Manager, then set the configuration settings in Listing Settings and the home page settings in Front Page Settings.

News Desk Action Summary:	Administrative Module:
1. Create News Category	NewsDesk – ARTICLES MGMT
2. Create News Article(s)	NewsDesk – ARTICLES MGMT
3. Set News InfoBox Home Page configuration settings	NewsDesk Mgmt – Front Page Settings
4. Set News InfoBox general	NewsDesk Mgmt – Listing Settings, FrontPage

listing configuration settings	Settings, Reviews Settings and Sticky Settings
5. Enable or disable News InfoBox to display	DESIGN CONTROLS – Infobox Admin – click GREEN button next to News Article.
6. Enable or disable a specific news article to display	NewsDesk MGMT – navigate to the News Article and click the GREEN button.
7. Administer your News Desk	NewsDesk - Reviews Mgmt

From the main Administrative Menu, select **News Desk – ARTICLES MGMT**. This brings you to the **Newsdesk Article Management menu.**

1. Create a News Category:

The example below has three sections entitled Sports News, Local News, and Neighborhood News. This might be appropriate for a local sports memorabilia website.

To add articles to the Sports News category, click the FILE FOLDER ⬜ and then select the **NEW NEWS ITEM** BUTTON.

 TIP: If you forget to click the FILE FOLDER and put your article in the wrong category, simply highlight the article and click MOVE.

NewsDesk... Category
And News Management

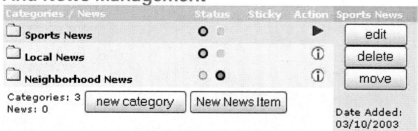

To **EDIT, DELETE or MOVE** a category, select it in the **ACTION** column and select either the **EDIT, DELETE or MOVE BUTTON.**

To **ADD** a new news category, click the **NEW CATEGORY button.**

2. Create a News Item:

To **ADD a new NEWS ITEM**, click the **NEW NEWS ITEM** button. This takes you to the **Add NEWS Story page.**

Add the headline, summary, text, images and settings as follows:

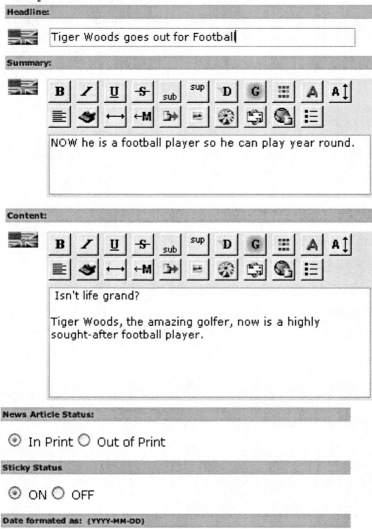

Start Date: 2004-09-30 ▽

URL to outside resource: (without http://)

▓▓▓ [   ]

Article Image(s):

First Image:

[   ] Browse...

Image title for First Image:

▓▓▓ [action   ]

newsdesk_test_osc_action.gif

Second Image:

[   ] Browse...

Image title for Second Image:

▓▓▓ [cartoons   ]

newsdesk_test_osc_cartoons.gif

4. News InfoBox General Listing Configuration Settings

This is the configuration page for the News Desk module. The default is shown below. It's not necessary to tweak these settings unless you wish to change them:

News Desk Listing Settings

Title	Value	Action	Search Results
Search Results	20	▶	
Page Links	5	ⓘ	[edit]
Display Headline	1	ⓘ	
Display Summary	1	ⓘ	How many articles do you
Display Content	1	ⓘ	want to list?
Display Date	1	ⓘ	
Display URL	1	ⓘ	Date Added: 02/16/2003
Display Status	1	ⓘ	
Display Image 1	1	ⓘ	
Display Image 2	1	ⓘ	
Display Image 3	1	ⓘ	
Location of Prev/Next Navigation Bar	3	ⓘ	

News Desk Front Page Settings

This menu sets the look of the News InfoBox on your Home Page. The default is shown below. It's not necessary to tweak these settings unless you wish to change them:

News Desk Front Page Settings

Title	Value	Action	Display Main News Items
Display Main News Items	3	▶	
Latest News Box Counts	5	ⓘ	[edit]
Display Latest News Box	1	ⓘ	
Display News Catagory Box	1	ⓘ	How many articles do you
Display View Counts	1	ⓘ	want to display on the top
Display Read More	1	ⓘ	page?

Display Summary	1	ⓘ
Display Headline	1	ⓘ
Display Date	1	ⓘ
Display Image 1	1	ⓘ
Display Image 2	1	ⓘ
Display Image 3	1	ⓘ

News Desk Reviews Settings

If you wish to enable or disable the display of reviews your customers write about each article, enable this module by clicking the EDIT BUTTON and entering 1 to enable and 0 to disable, then clicking the UPDATE button:

News Desk Reviews Settings

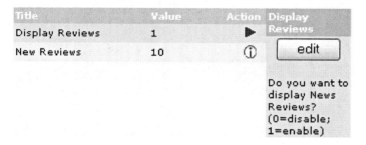

Number of News Reviews to Display

To change the number of reviews that are automatically displayed about each News article, enable this module by clicking the item in the ACTION column, entering the number of reviews you want to display, then clicking the UPDATE button.

News Desk Reviews Settings

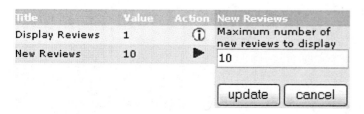

News Desk Sticky Settings

To change the settings for the items that remain at the top of your News Articles section (STICKY items), from the **main Administrative Menu**, select **NewsDesk – STICKY SETTINGS.**

Below are the default values; to change, simply click the **Action** column and then click the **EDIT button:**

News Desk Sticky Settings

Title	Value	Action	Display Headline
Display Headline	1	►	edit
Display Summary	1	ⓘ	
Display Content	1	ⓘ	Do you want to display the
Display View Counts	1	ⓘ	headline?
Display Read More	1	ⓘ	(0=disable; 1=enable)
Display Date	1	ⓘ	
Display URL	1	ⓘ	Date Added:
Display Image	1	ⓘ	03/02/2003
Display Image 2	1	ⓘ	
Display Image 3	1	ⓘ	

5. Enable or disable the News InfoBox to display

From the main Administrative Menu shown on p. 12, under Design Controls select Infobox Admin. This brings up the **Infobox Display, Create and Update menu.**

To ENABLE the News Infobox, click the GREEN BUTTON next to NewsDesk. To DISABLE, click the RED BUTTON:

Title	Font Color	Activate Box?	Set Column	Box Template	Position
NewsDesk		○ ●	◄ ►	infobox	⬆ ⬇

6. Enable or disable a specific news article to display

To show or hide a news article, from the main Administrative Menu, select NEWSDESK – Articles Mgmt. This brings you to the NewsDesk Category and News Management Menu:

NewsDesk ... Category and News Management

Categories / News	Date	Status	Sticky	Action
Tiger Woods HOT NEWS!	2004-09-29 23:07:09	⊙ ⚬	⚬ ⊙	▶

Simply click the GREEN button next to your News Article to enable it; click the RED button to disable it.

To make the news article stay at the top of the news list, even after you add more news articles, click the GREEN button under "STICKY"; the RED button to un-stick it.

7. Administer your News Desk: Reviews Management

If you wish to enable or disable the display of reviews your customers write about each article, enable this module by clicking the EDIT BUTTON and entering 1 to enable and 0 to disable, then clicking the UPDATE button.

News Article Reviews

Articles	Rating	Date Added	Approved	Action	NewsDesk version 1.4
NewsDesk version 1.4	★★★★★	03/11/2003	⊙	▶	edit
3 images !!!	★★★★★	03/11/2003	⊙	ⓘ	delete
Stickies are here!	★★★★★	03/11/2003	⊙	ⓘ	Approve

To edit a review, simply highlight it in the **ACTION column** and then click the **EDIT BUTTON. You will see the same screen that the customer saw.**

Make your edits and click PREVIEW:

News Article Reviews

Article:
From: Carsten aka Moyashi

Date: 03/11/2003
Review:

hehe, after almost a week of effort I was able to finish this
part of the mod.

I hope that you all enjoy it!

NOTE: HTML is not translated!

Rating: BAD ○ ○ ○ ◉ ○ GOOD

[preview] [cancel]

Chapter

5

Technical Details

In this chapter:

CRE Loaded osCommerce 6.1 is structured similarly to standard osCommerce, but with some notable exceptions. If you're a new user you can probably ignore this chapter; it is provided for those tech-types who love to know about the guts of the program they are using.

Level of difficulty: medium, depending on your interest & experience.

CRE Loaded osCommerce 6.15 File Structure

Standard ms2.2 osCommerce

Name ▲
- 📁 admin
- 📁 download
- 📁 images
- 📁 includes
- 📁 pub

CRE Loaded 6.15

Name ▲
- 📁 admin
- 📁 doc
- 📁 download
- 📁 images
- 📁 includes
- 📁 temp
- 📁 templates
- 📁 tmp

*Note: the INSTALL directory, included in both of the original packages, are not show here because they are removed immediately after installation for security reasons.

CRE Loaded osCommerce 6.1 contains *hundreds* of files that standard osCommerce does not. However, the program adheres as closely as possible to the original file structure. You can see that the top level file structure is almost identical, except for:

DOC: Documentation and README files (equivalent to osCommerce's PUB Folder).

TEMP and TMP: Used to speed temporary uploads and downloads in database backup and restore, and in uploading or downloading the product database using the EasyPopulate feature.

TEMPLATES: Changes that affect ALL pages are filed here, and updated in the Adminstrative Menu, rather than having to make manual coding edits on dozens of pages.

If you are accustomed to making all you manual coding edits in the directory **/includes/languages/english/*.php**, you will need to first ask yourself:

Does this coding change affect ALL PAGES?	→ If so, it is probably done in the TEMPLATES directory.
Does this coding change affect SEVERAL PAGES, such as a SECTION (ie. Affiliates, Checkout)?	→ If so, it is probably done in the TEMPLATES/CONTENT directory.
Does this coding change affect a SINGLE PAGE?	→ If so, you will probably do it in the same directory, includes/languages/english/*.php.

TIP: Don't get frustrated looking for files you want to edit. Instead, use SEARCH to find a bit of text or code you KNOW will be on the page.

New Locations of Files Originally Found in /includes/languages/english/ - now look in:

templates	Original	images	buttons	english
	main_page.tpl.php	logo.gif		ALL YOUR BUTTONS
	boxes.tpl.php	oscommerce.gif		
	content			
	Content that displays in ALL TEMPLATES			

Template File Detail:

**templates/Original – the Default osCommerce "look" template
main_page.tpl.php – edit your header, footer, body
boxes.tpl.php – edit the look of ALL InfoBoxes
logo.gif – your company logo
oscommerce.gif – the original osCommerce logo
templates/Original/images/buttons/english: where all your buttons are now.**

PHP Coding Details

If you wish to delve into the page code and really customize osCommerce, you can make it easy on yourself if you use a PHP Editor such as Dreamweaver, PHP Edit, PHP Coder, etc. This will highlight the code in different colors so you can immediately see where problems lie. A code comparison program like Beyond Compare will also make your comparisons a breeze.

Here are the coding tips you will need to make reading and editing the code a little easier:

PHP Commands	Example of Usage:

Single-line Comment // or # prevents php from reading that line, easy way to "remove" an infobox that you may later replace	`// we've just hidden this`
	`line of code`
	
	`# this line is also hidden.`

Multi-Line Comments /* */	`/* everything between these`
	`start and    end comment`
	`codes is hidden. */`

Escape Character or Backslash \ prevents PHP from delivering an error message when it sees	`What\'s New Here?`

Start and End PHP in 3 different formats
 	
Normally lower case, some servers (ie RedHat) may have trouble with the middle format
	`<?php   code here;    ?>`
	
	`<?      code here;    ?>`
	
	`<script language="php">`
	`code here </script>`

The PHP End Statement Like a period in English, the ; tells PHP that the statement is complete	`<?php code here; ?>`

PHP Echo Function ECHO ( ) Writes the content between quotation marks into a generated HTML page	`<?php`
	`echo( "What\'s New Here?"`
	`); ?>`

PHP Rule: NO extra spaces or lines.	Unlike HTML, PHP cannot handle extra spaces or lines. Remove them!
Newline: moves to a new line in text areas like 	The quick brown fox \n jumped over the lazy dog.
Double newline: moves down two new lines as in <p>	Knock, knock. \n\n Who is there?
Tab: moves text horizontally in the text area.	Donuts are not good for you. \n\n \t\t\t Signed, your Mother.

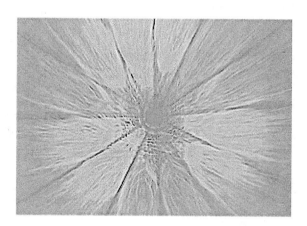

Installation or Upgrade of CRE Loaded 6.1 to 6.15

In this chapter:

osCommerce CRE Loaded 6.15 is easier than ever to install. Use a web host that specializes in osCommerce and they will probably install it for you, for FREE.

If you simply must do it yourself because you can, even when free and easy alternatives exist, I'm happy to say this install is the easiest ever.

Level of difficulty: easy for someone who likes this stuff.

If you use a web host that specializes in osCommerce hosting, you won't need to worry about a thing:

- You KNOW they have the latest PHP, Apache, and MySQL support up to date.
- Their servers will not be slow.
- Their databases will be optimized for e-commerce.
- You will know they have the equipment it takes to support critical financial transactions.
- Their tech support will be top-notch.
- Support will understand what you are talking about when you call to ask a question.
- MANY OF THEM WILL INSTALL OSCOMMERCE FOR YOU FOR FREE.
- MANY WILL TRANSFER YOUR OLD OSCOMMERCE SITE FROM ANOTHER HOST FOR FREE.
- It's a great way to get into the guts of the program and decide if it's right for you without getting sidetracked by the installation process.

TIP: This author recommends using ONLY web hosts that *specialize in osCommerce hosting.*

1. *Free* Installation at Chain Reaction Web:

Chain Reaction is the *maker* of CRE Loaded 6.1 osCommerce. *No host knows more about the product than they do.*

Chain Reaction Web provides real full time support for use or support issues via phone or email 24/7 from the makers of the CRE loaded 6 oscommerce and the most experience oscommerce hosting provider. They have the optimal setup for osCommerce, including:

- Most updated version of osCommerce CRE Loaded with all patches pre-installed, if any
- All Demo Data Removed
- Complete Install of Catalog and Admin, all directories and folders created
- File write permissions set
- Installation Choice of store installed 'As Home Page' or 'In Catalog folder'
- Unlimited osCommerce support from Chain Reaction Web
- mySQL database and user access setup
- Latest phpMyAdmin to edit your database

- PHP (with register global's on :)
- FREE SSL Server Access (your entire site is covered)
- FREE HTTPS shared certificate ($125.00 value)
- 125 MB dedicated file storage; mysql, logs files and email stored separately
- 7 GB of data transfer
- Solid FreeBSD UNIX Servers
- Choice of location in one of our multiple Data centers
- OC 48 Fiber Optic Backbone
- Free Urchin Site Stats
- We guarantee the setup of a hosting account within 1 business day of your order, or the setup fee will be waived.
  Setup Guarantee does not apply to add ons and other services.
- They guarantee the uptime of our servers and the performance of their server software, or you receive a free month of hosting
- Customer Support Guarantee: they guarantee your satisfaction with response time and the quality of support you receive, or you receive a free month of hosting.

Installation Instructions for CRE Loaded at Chain Reaction Web:

1. **Decide on domain name. If you wish, you may register it yourself but if you haven't, let Chain Reaction Web register it for you.**
2. **Click this link and fill in the form:**

http://www.chainreactionweb.com/info/hosting/shared_dev_php_site.php

That's it! [†]

2. Standard Installation on your own web host:

Before you begin, fill **out the Pre-Installation Checklist** completely. This will allow you to have all the information you will need during installation and configuration in one place. This will save you many, many hours of back-and-forth figuring out little, "just-one-more" things that were staring you in the face all along.

[†] Yes, this is a "shameless plug" by this author for Chain Reaction Web. But they created this program, for heavens sakes! They provide unlimited technical support! Who could possibly help you better when things go wrong?

Pre-Installation Checklist:

1. Supporting Programs Needed on Your Personal Computer

☐ **FTP (File Transfer Protocol) program** to upload files, create directories and set file permissions. See p.2 of this guide for some suggestions.

☐ WinZip (PC) or Windows XP (WinZip is pre-installed)

☐ (Recommended) A **code comparison program** such as Beyond Compare www.scootersoftware.com – Free Trial.

☐ (Optional) Site management/HTML editor program like **Dreamweaver** to synchronize [create a mirror website on your PC] and quick Search [CTRL-F] to locate the code you wish to edit)

☐ (Optional) If you don't use Dreamweaver, a **PHP editor/ debugger** such as PHPEdit, PHP Coder 3, highlights code in different colors, easy to see coding errors

2. Hosting Information
Ask your Web Host for this info

☐ What version of PHP and MySQL does your web host use/support?

☐ What kind of servers does your web host use? (Apache, etc.)

☐ What tools (i.e. cPanel) does your web host for database creation and account administration?

☐ Does your web host support phpMyAdmin for administering your database? If not, what do they use or recommend for database creation and administration?

☐ Does your web host back up your website files? How often? Your database? How often? How do you have files restored?

3. Secure Server Info:
Ask your Web Host for this info

☐ What is the internal path to your secure server?

☐ What is the internal path to your secure images directory?

☐ Does your web host offer a shared SSL certificate, or will you purchase your own SSL certificate? (Note, you may not need your own— check with your payment processor first)

4. Database Info:
Ask your Web Host for this info

☐ What is the Hostname or IP address of your database server?

☐ What is your exact database username?

☐ What full-rights password does your database use?

☐ What is the name of your database (not database username)?

☐ Have the database and username been linked?

☐ Is there a secondary database username and password with more restrictions which offers more security?

5. Domain Name/Location:
Ask your Web Host for this info

- [ ] Do you have your domain name registered?
- [ ] What is the exact www address?

- [ ] Did you register it at least 24-72 hours ago?Type the address in your browser to be sure it is live.
- [ ] Have you notified your web host about your new domain name so they can "point" your files to it?
- [ ] What is the full path to your Web Server Root Directory? (Ask your web host, it will be like /usr/www/users/yourname/html/)
- [ ] Is there a secondary database username and password with more restrictions which offers more security?

6. Other Information:

- [ ] What payment gateway will you use? What is their URL, Username, account number, and password?
- [ ] What shipping company will you use? What is their URL, Username, account number, and password?
- [ ] Are you required to charge tax? On what products, what rate, and in what regions? Get help from your attorney.

TIP: To help you select payment and shipping carriers, a 40-page special report "Payment & Shipping Comparisons" is available from oscommercemanuals.com. Includes bonus chapter on disaster prevention and recovery.

Now that you have all the answers to the Pre-Installation Checklist, Alex, read ahead for the questions.

Install It Yourself:

Check off each item as you complete it.

☐ 1. Get your *free* copy of CRE Loaded 6.15

Download the most recent version of osCommerce CRE Loaded from www.creloaded.com – click the **DOWNLOADS** link in the left column. Select the **FULL DOWNLOAD. Or the direct link is http://creloaded.com/Downloads/d_op=viewdownload/cid=1.html** title is "CRE loaded 6.15."

Which Package should I get - Windows or Linux/UNIX?
If you need to ask, the Windows version ZIP file is right for you. These instructions are for the Windows version.

☐ 2. Unzip the files onto your PC

Double-Click the Zip file name (Windows XP) or use WinZip or a similar zip program to unzip your files into the folder on your personal computer where you will administer and manage your website. A good place is to make a new folder called My Store in the My Documents folder.

☐ 3. Upload the files to your web host

If you don't have an FTP program, get a free or trial version such as CuteFTP or similar FTP program. There will be a "Wizard" to walk you through setting it up for your website. **Use the settings from your Pre-Installation Checklist.**

CuteFTP www.cuteftp.com

CoffeecupFTP
www.coffeecup.com

Upload all the files into your ROOT directory (see your Pre-Installation Checklist).

TIP: There are over 1,600 files to upload. If you are on dial-up or satellite uplink, it may take you hours to upload! Try starting your upload before bedtime.

TIP: If you will only use one of the default languages, you can safely delete one or two of the other default language directories (/espanol/ or /german/) to reduce your upload time.

TIP: Make sure ALL your files get uploaded! If all the files do not upload completely, your install may not be successful and/or the program may not function normally. It is difficult to track down this problem, so it is best to be certain to prevent it. Either "synchronize" using a site manager like Dreamweaver or FrontPage, or upload twice using your FTP program.

IMPORTANT: DOUBLE-CHECK to make sure all the files uploaded completely. Your installation will not succeed if any file is missing. This is one of the MOST COMMON INSTALLATION PROBLEMS.

☐ 4. Temporarily Set File Permissions to 706**

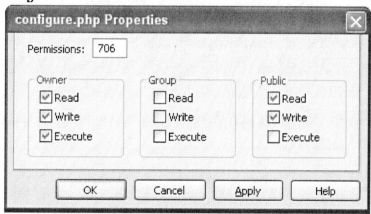

Using your **Pre-Installation Checklist** and your **FTP PROGRAM** or your web host's web-based **administration tool** (not osCommerce's), you are now going to change the file permissions on the 2 following configuration files.

An FTP Program with permissions set to 706.

In CuteFTP, enter your ftp website address (usually ftp.yourdomain.com), start by entering your FTP username and password that your web host gave you, and the path to your domain's folder.

To set permissions, from your domain's root (usually public_html), double-click the folder INCLUDES to open it, then find and RIGHT-click on the file configure.php. From the drop-down menu that appears, select PROPERTIES and change the permissions as described and shown in the picture below. Repeat this procedure for the other configure file.

```
/includes/configure.php
/admin/includes/configure.php
```

***SECURITY WARNING:** Set permissions initially to 706. *Change it to 777 ONLY if the program gives an error message telling you that the permissions need to be changed.* You MUST change the permissions again after installation for security reasons.

TIP: Leave your FTP program open **while you move on to the Installation section in case you need to change some additional permissions.**

☐ 5. Create your database

Use **phpMyAdmin, cPanel,** or **your web host's web-based database administration tool** to:
1. **Create an empty database**
2. **Create a user, and**
3. **Assign a user to the database.**

Each web host will use a different or even custom database administration tool, so check out their support section or contact them for specific directions on how to use it.

After Database Setup: .

Once you have created your empty database, you will receive an information screen with the exact database name, server location, and your username and password. **SAVE AND PRINT THIS DATABASE INFORMATION** and keep it in a safe place – you will need it for the next step.

☐ 6. Begin installing the CRE Loaded program

Using your web browser, go to the following address:
http://www.yourdomainname.com/install/

Please refer to your **Pre-Installation Checklist** for each item on the following Installation screens.

TIP: If your domain name is new, it may not be active yet – it can take up to 72 hours. Instead, you will have to use your "IP Address" to install the program. Ask your web host for your site's exact IP address.

If you are copying and pasting information into your install screens, and have trouble, check to be sure you are not pasting extra SPACES at the beginning or end of the words.

Install Step 1.
Welcome
Screen

Click the "Install" icon at the bottom of this screen to begin automatic installation.:

Install Step 2.
New Installation
Screen

Click the ? for helpful details about each selection. osCommerce pre-selects the default values for you; **do not change them unless you know what you are doing.**

Click the **"Continue" Button.**

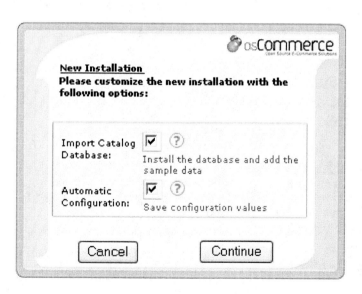

Install Step 3. Database Server Information

This screen is not filled in for you. Copy the database information from your Pre-Install Checklist.

When you think it's right, click the **"Continue" Button.**

The installation program will test it for you.

You might get it wrong a few times – especially database SERVER (usually a number) and database NAME (usually a name).

Install Step 4. Database Import Screen

Don't worry, you can't break it! Just hit your browser's BACK button, switch the information and try again.

Click the **"Continue" Button.**

Install Step 5.
Database
Import Success

Good job! Click the
"Continue" Button.

Install Step 6.
Database
Server
Information

osCommerce pre-
selects the default
values for you; **do not
change them unless
you know what you
are doing.**
Click the **"Continue"
Button.**

Install Step 7. Admin Password Configuration Screen

Enter your current email address. You will use this email address every time you log on, and the system will test to be sure it is a valid address. If you ever lose your password, you can click "Password Forgotten?" and a new password will be mailed to this email address.

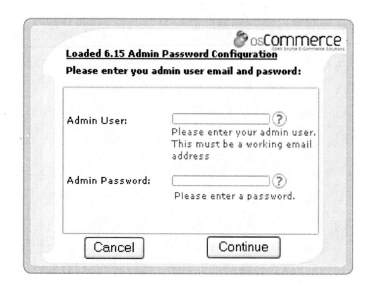

Enter a new password that you can remember, and keep it in a safe place.

Install Step 8. Installation Success Screen CONGRATULATIONS!

Click the CATALOG Button to see your new store!

Then click the ADMINISTRATION TOOL and log on with the info you entered in Step 7 to begin setting up your store.

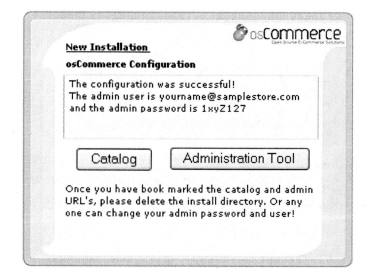

If you had any trouble, go back and check each of the items on the Pre-Installation Checklist, then check your steps beginning with Step 1. If you find that you have done each step correctly, turn to the Installation Troubleshooting section.

 If you receive an error message about permissions, go back to Setting File Permissions and increase the file permissions to 777 using your FTP program before returning to this screen and clicking RETRY. Remember you MUST change them back after installation.

☐ 7. Set Security and Permissions.

Using your FTP program for all items in this section, you MUST do the following:

 SECURITY WARNING: You MUST delete the Install folder AND change the permissions on your configuration files as instructed, or your store will be a security risk.

	Do this:	To the following folder:
A	**For security,** DELETE the Install folder. If you ever need it again you can re-upload it from your personal computer: (RIGHT-click it, then select DELETE from the drop-down menu):	`install`
B	**For security,** change configuration file permissions **to 644** so only you, the owner, can read and write, and all others can read-only.‡:	`/includes/configure.php`
C	**So the program can upload your Main Page (home page) text** for you, set the file permissions **to 706** on this file:	`/includes/languages/english/mainpage.php`
D	**To allow the program to upload images you select,**	`/images/`

	change the images file permissions **to 706** on this FOLDER:	
E	**So the program will be permitted to write backups**, set the file permissions on the backups directory **to 706:**	`/admin/backups`
F	**To allow the program to write graphs**, change the directory file permissions **to 706:**	`/admin/images/` `/admin/images/graphs`
G	**For security**, change ADMIN configuration file permissions **to 644** so only you, the owner, can read and write, and all others can read-only.[§]:	`admin/includes/configure.php`
H	**So the program can upload images** to the templates directory, change the file permissions **to 706** on this FOLDER (or other template folder if you change from Original template)	`/templates/Original/images/` or `/templates/(templatename)/images/`
I	**So you can batch-upload products** with EasyPopulate, change the file permissions **to 706** on this FOLDER:	`/temp/`

Installation Problem-Solving

If you've had any difficulty with your installation, check again to be sure that you have set the appropriate file permissions for each folder or directory that requires it. That usually fixes 99% of installation problems.

[§] If you continue to receive permissions warnings, try setting configure.php to read-only, 444. This warning is due to the security settings on some web hosts' servers. Check with your web host for more information.

If you still have difficulty, the osCommerce Technical Manual contains solutions to the top 25 osCommerce errors. See the **back of this book for more information.**

Technical Help Procedure:

1. **Read your Manual.**
2. **Ask your email group for more help, such as** <u>osCommerce-Newbies@yahoogroups.com</u>
3. **Go to the technical forums and FAQ for a similar problem** (<u>www.creloaded.com</u>)
4. **When all else fails, pay for technical support (or get free support from** <u>chainreactionweb.com</u>**, if you are a web hosting customer or wish to become one).**

B. Upgrade from Previous 6.1 Version to 6.15:

This CRE Loaded UPDATE procedure will upgrade CRE loaded 6.1 and CRE loaded 6.1a stores to CRE loaded 6.15. It is designed to read your existing configure.php file for information about your database, and install the changes to the database in the background.

If you have installed any of the patch 01 release candidates, please install this final version over it.

WARNING: These changes are created and tested based on an *un-modified, stock install of CRE loaded6.1a*. CONTRIBUTIONS OR MODIFICATIONS YOU HAVE ADDED MAY NOT FUNCTION PROPERLY AFTER ADDING THIS PATCH. Chainreactionweb and Members of the coding team are not responsible for any problems this patch causes you.

WARNING: Always use BEST PRACTICES when modifying your store: You MUST do a test install to a TEST STORE (copy of your live store), and if successful make a FULL BACKUP of your entire store and database before installing to your LIVE STORE.

Check off each item below as you complete it:

☐ 1. Get Your Upgrade File:

Download your CRE Loaded UPGRADE File from www.creloaded.com – click the **DOWNLOADS** link in the left column. Select **MAIN/MAIN RELEASES. Find "CRE Loaded 6.1 UPGRADE to 6.15" and save to your computer.**

Which Package should I get - Windows or Linux/UNIX?
If you need to ask, the Windows version ZIP file is right for you. These instructions are for the Windows version.

☐ 2. Unzip the Upgrade Files onto your PC:

Double-Click the Zip file name (Windows XP) or use WinZip or a similar zip program to unzip your files into the folder on your personal computer to a separate directory from you website files. We will assume for these instructions that you have put them in your c:\My Documents\Upgrade\ folder.

☐ 3. Review the list of files that have changed, bug fixes and contributions added.

On your personal computer, open the file c:\My Documents\Upgrade\doc\changes.txt *and* c:\My Documents\Upgrade\doc\changesloaded615.txt carefully review and compare them to your customized cart to see if there are any differences.

☐ 4. Upload the files to your web host

If you don't have an FTP program, get a free or trial version such as CuteFTP or similar FTP program. There will be a "Wizard" to walk you through setting it up for your website. Ask your web host if you need any help with settings.

CuteFTP
www.cuteftp.com

CoffeecupFTP
www.coffeecup.com

☐ 5. Set permissions on the temporary directory /tmp/ to 706.

To set permissions, from your domain's root (usually public_html), find and RIGHT-click on the NEW directory /tmp/. From the drop-down menu that appears, select PROPERTIES, and change the permissions to 706 .

SECURITY WARNING: **Set permissions initially to 706. *Change it to 777 ONLY if the program gives an error message telling you that the permissions need to be changed.* **You MUST change the permissions again after installation for security reasons.**

☐ 6. Create a Test Store with same configuration as your store and test it to be sure changes are functioning properly.

SINCE THIS PROGRAM IS FREE, CREATING A TEST STORE IS FREE. WHY RISK SKIPPING THIS STEP? TAKE A LITTLE TIME NOW, OR A LOTS AND LOTS OF TIME LATER... YOUR CHOICE.

☐ 7. Make a full backup copy of all your store files onto your personal computer using your FTP program.

TIP: Leave your FTP program open while you move on to the next few sections in case you need to change some permissions.

☐ 8. Make a full backup copy of your database using phpMyAdmin.

TIP: If you have never used phpMyAdmin before, get the electronic manual, "Using phpMyAdmin with osCommerce" from osCommerceManuals.com.

☐ 9. Delete the following files:

- ☐ /Order_Info.php
- ☐ /Order_Info_Process.php
- ☐ /templates/content/Order_Info.tpl.php
- ☐ /templates/content/Order_Info_Process.tpl.php

If you prefer, you can change the names of these files rather than deleting, i.e. "Order_Info-61a.php.

☐ 10. If you are using the generic "Credit Card" payment module:

- ☐ Go into the Admin MODULES – Payment, Credit Card, and print a copy of your settings.
- ☐ UNINSTALL the generic "Credit Card" Module.

TIP: Steps 9 and 10 are to correct a capitalization problem with filenames in this module. If you use the generic "Credit Card" payment module but skip this step, the capitalization problems will NOT be corrected.

☐ 11. IF YOU HAVE MADE *ANY* CHANGES to your stock store files:

COMPARE the changes using an automatic comparison program like Beyond Compare (scootersoftware.com) and manually merge files you have changed, rather then copying over the originals.

OR, IF YOU HAVE NOT made changes to your stock store files:

Use your FTP program to upload and replace all the files in the patch to the catalog. The files are FULL FILE REPLACEMENTS and are nested in their correct directories.

☐ 12. Install the changes to the database:
☐ **Run the script http://www.yourstorename.com/patch/index.php** to add the required fields to the mySQL database.

Updates to the **admin_files table** should be added, **whos_online** has 1 field added and **on configuration**
entry so you can pick which product list to use, should be added only if they are not already in the database.
It will also check to make sure you are not using the **default user and password**. If you are, you MUST change them quickly as this is a security risk.

OR, if you prefer,

☐ Use **phpMyAdmin** to manually install the changes to the database.

☐ 13. Delete the /patch/ directory and all files in this directory.

WARNING: Failure to delete the /patch/ directory will compromise the security of your site.

☐ 14. Delete the file /includes/modules/payment/cc.php

☐ 15. (Optional) Reinstall Credit Card or Credit Card with CCV "Credit Card Verification" checking.

TIP: "CCV" is a fraud-protection program; you may need to pay your credit card processor extra to use this setting.

If you removed and need to replace Credit Card, go to **MODULES – PAYMENT – Credit Card** or **Credit Card with CCV** and click **INSTALL**.

16. Familiarize Yourself with Admin Changes in this Version.

Two of the biggest changes are:

1. **DEFINE MAINPAGE is moved to Info System** menu from Catalog menu.

2. **Dynamic DROP-DOWN Admin Menus** (DHTML Admin Menus) may be enabled from the **CONFIGURATION – MY STORE – Enable DHTML Menu.**

If you would like the drop-down menus to appear in the Admin like the picture to the right, change this setting to TRUE.

Turn ON Drop-Down
ADMIN Menus

Upgrade Problem-Solving

If you've had any difficulty with your upgrade, check again to be sure that you have set the appropriate file permissions for each folder or directory that requires it. That usually fixes 99% of installation problems.

If you still have difficulty, please go to the CRE Forums at www.creloaded.com for problem-solving help.

APPENDIX A
About Chain Reaction Web Hosting
http://www.chainreactionweb.com

The CRE Loaded release of osCommerce is developed and maintained by Chain Reaction Web. Chain Reaction Web's primary business is providing tier 1 quality web hosting at low cost to small to medium size businesses. While not cheap compared to some hosting companies, Chain Reaction Web offers a higher end hosting platform that only top level providers such as those that actually own their own data centers can provide. This is because Chain Reaction Web uses NTT/Verio as its infrastructure provider. NTT/Verio provides Chain Reaction Web with fully managed servers, monitoring and security updates. This allows Chan Reaction Web to focus on supporting the applications that are hosted on the server.

We do osCommerce hosting with the highest level of uptime and performance. In order to provide hosting to for osCommerce and other business applications, the highest level of uptime and performance must be maintenance. Unfortunately the market is overrun with companies that say 100% uptime and great support, etc. To prove the point of its commitment to actually deliver uptime, stability and quality effective support Chain Reaction Web does business month to month, without pre-pays or contracts. We also guarantee all three aspects of hosting, uptime, performance, and support, each and every month. Almost all other hosting companies only provide a guarantee for the first 30 days due to their long contracts and prepays. Chain Reaction Web will refund your money for a given month no matter how long a customer host with them. If you're not happy, you don't pay for that month.

Why do we develop the CRE Loaded release of osCommerce? We do it because it needs to be done, and we see the increase return on investment by meeting this need. Not only does it make our own hosting customer more profitable to have these features, we release it as open source so anyone can benefit from it. In the end Chain Reaction Web benefits from the good will of the community and the reputation of knowing osCommerce so well that we can deliver the CRE Loaded as an ongoing stable release. There is no doubt that osCommerce store owners turn to Chain Reaction Web when they realize that hosting osCommerce is not the same as hosting an HTML page or a simply php script. While there are many that download the CRE Loaded host it elsewhere, we believe that since osCommerce was available to use for free and we have been able to build our business around it, we are only giving back to the community by developing the CRE Loaded.

The future of the osCommerce market. We see the osCommerce and open source hosting as a growing market and we welcome innovate and value driven companies as well as recognize the companies that have been in this market the entire time. Chain Reaction Web has been forming partnerships with the leading template, merchant, accounting companies that bring the best product and services to the osCommerce store owner. Also the CRE Loaded project is maturing into a better organized open source project and we are working implement better tools to assist the developers and the community with the implementation of source forge bug tracking and more links to help in the admin of the latest release.

For those interested in hosting or customizations to your CRE Loaded application here some information about our services.

About our services

Secure Shared Hosting begins at 19.99 a month, includes sure checkout and osCommerce preinstalled. Secure Virtual Private Servers start at 59.99, with the latest technology VPS v2 starting at 149.99 per month. Bandwidth is unmetered and we provider free unlimited support for osCommerce, Zen-Cart and any stable php/mysql application to all our hosting customers. www.chainreactionweb.com/info/manual/

Customization services cost range from $50 - $400 for contribution installations. We have engaged in large scale customizations of osCommerce that range in price from $500 - $5,000. We have a professional project manager, all our pricing is fixed, never hourly, and we warranty all our work for the lifetime of the code.

We routinely provide the following services to our osCommerce customers and others that host elsewhere: Template Modification, altering an existing template that is already installed and active on a site Template Creation, converting html and graphics into a template and installing it Payment Module Configuration, installing and configuring a payment module and testing Creation of Payment and Shipping Modules, 'nuff said. Product Import, importing data from non-standard data sources, Store Conversations, Converting old osCommerce and other loaded brand stores to the latest CRE Loaded.

Contact projects@chainreactionweb.com with a detailed description of what you need for a free fixed cost estimate and time line.

Partner Links:
www.algozone.com (http://www.algozone.com/shop/default.php?ref=2)
www.stoneedge.com
www.osCommercemanuals.com
http://www.itwebsolution.com/

Resources:
Ecommerce Exchange Authorize.net Provider
(https://freecreditcardprocessing.com/applynow/online_application.asp?code=chainrea
ction)

APPENDIX B
About the osCommerce Manuals Library:

The osCommerce Users Manual V2.0

Shows you everything you can do yourself using the Administrative Module, once the program is installed (and we can refer you to hosts who will install your site FOR FREE).

Our exclusive **QUICK START GUIDE** can help you get your first osCommerce Website up and running in as little as 30 minutes after installation.

Nearly 50 new pages have been added to Version 2.0, including:

- **Review and comparison of Credit Card Payment Processors** so you can easily choose the best one for your company's needs. Includes fees, countries available, length of commitment, and ease of installation.
- **Shipping Methods comparison** to make selecting the right shipper easy.
- **ALL NEW CHAPTER - Records and Database Management,** Disaster Planning & Recovery. Hurricane Ivan, we've got you covered.

INCLUDES LINKS TO OUR EXCLUSIVE, WEB-BASED FREE CHECKLISTS and CHEATSHEETS to make managing your new store a breeze, including:

- **List of Web Hosts, Installers & Consultants - many will install or move your store for FREE**
- **PRE-SETUP Checklist for Your Store**
- **Font and Color Selectors**
- **Look and Feel Checklist**
- **InfoBox Checklist**
- **Greetings Checklist**
- **Advanced Users' Fully-Commented Style Sheet**
- **Advanced Users' Annotated Cheat Sheet**

These checklists may be used by osCommerce consultants, installers and web hosts to zip through your installations.

See more info and get your copy today at:
http://www.oscommercemanuals.com/product_info.php?products_id=29

About the osCommerce Manuals Library:

The osCommerce Technical Manual

Shows you everything you can do yourself using the Administrative Module, once the program is installed (and we can refer you to hosts who will install your site FOR FREE).

Shows the web developer in Non-Tech-speak, plain-English, step-by-step instructions for everything you need to install, configure, customize, install add-on contributions, and troubleshoot your own ecommerce store, including:

- **Standard Installation**
- **Setting up Store at Root Level**
- **Installing to a Secure SSL Server**
- **Moving a Site to a NEW Server**
- **Website Security**
- **About PHP and MySQL**
- **Setting Up Your Own Testing Site**
- **(Optional) Installing PHP, MySQL, Apache, phpMyAdmin**
- **osCommerce Product Architecture**
- **Advanced Fun with Text**
- **Advanced Fun with Emails**
- **Advanced Fun with Colors & Graphics, and**
- **Other Customizations.**

SPECIAL BONUS MATERIALS INCLUDED:
PRE-*INSTALLATION* CHECKLIST

Our exclusive checklist can help you get your first osCommerce Website up and running in as little as 30 minutes after file upload!
PRE-*LAUNCH* TESTING CHECKLIST
Helps you quickly run through your entire website to KNOW it is free of errors before launch.
TOP 25 ERRORS AND SOLUTIONS
No need to waste hours of frustration sweating out the answers; they are almost surely in this bonus guide. Non-Tech-speak, plain-English, step-by-step instructions on how to solve it. User-friendly IS spoken here.
TOP 16 ADD-ON CONTRIBUTIONS
REVIEWS AND INSTALLATION INFO

See more info and get your copy today at:
http://www.oscommercemanuals.com/product_info.php?products_id=32

INDEX

ondemandmanuals.com
A division of Trafford Holdings Ltd.

This manual is made available to users of this software by Pithy Productions through On Demand Manuals.

Ordering Copies of this Manual:

This manual can be ordered online at www2.ondemandmanuals.com/pithy
You may also email an order for this manual to ODMorders@trafford.com, quoting catalogue #04-2373

For any questions about purchasing or use of this software, contact Pithy Productions directly.

ISBN 1-41204565-7

9 781412 045650

10 9 8 7 6 5 4 3